Searching FOR A DEEPER *Love*

REGINA LEWIS-MARTIN

ISBN 979-8-88943-909-7 (paperback)
ISBN 979-8-88943-910-3 (digital)

Christian Faith Publishing
832 Park Avenue
Meadville, PA 16335
www.christianfaithpublishing.com

Printed in the United States of America

In memory

Robert T. Lewi, father
Cloria M. Lewis, mother
Henry N. Frost, daddy
Emerson Cain, grandfather
Elizabeth Cain, grandmother
Mary Green, aunt (Cloria's sister)
Sissy Griffin, great-grandmother (Emerson's mother)
Era Bell Richardson, great-grandmother (Elizabeth's mother)

Although you're gone, you'll never be forgotten.
What each of you placed in me, I hold it dear and near my heart.

Contents

Preface

I dedicate this book to all who had a hand in structuring and nurturing my life. Too many to name, but you know who you are. I'm dedicated to my purpose, which is to do the will of God. We must know that using the vessel for the wrong purpose is being abused, or allowing yourself to be abused, because you're not in the right position of purpose. What went wrong was right to get you in position to be the vessel that He designed you to be—the king that is in you, the queen that is in you, the victor that is in you. Keep laboring, for the harvest is near. Through this process, you will get to the promise. Do it God's way. Stay in the will of God. If you want the promise of Christ, you must live the life of Christ. Your thoughts equal your words; your words equal your attitude; your attitude equals your behavior; your behavior equals your character. When life gets harder, we must become stronger by reading and living God's Word.

Al Green said, "Love and happiness. Love will make you do wrong. Love will make you do right. Love will make you come home early. Love will make you stay out all night long." But I say, to be dedicated to love, you must know God, for God is love. If you don't know God, then you don't know love. Stay dedicated to God, and don't worry about any setbacks, for God has made a way for your comeback. For every failure, God has made a way for restoration. For all ashes, God has made a way for the beauties of the Lord. For every disappointment, God has made a way for a new beginning. Don't worry about the mistakes, for we all have sinned and come short of the glory of God. Just stay focused on God, be dedicated to God, and know that His mercy is new every morning. You must know that where the Spirit of the Lord is, there is liberty.

You might be a product of your past, but know this: you don't have to be a prisoner of your past. God orchestrates the plans of our life. Jesus, who changes not, went away to prepare a place for His prepared people. Stay dedicated and in a position as a good soldier. We must endure this hardship just like Jesus when He was faced with the hardship of carrying our sins on the cross. His flesh prayed to God, His Father, to take this bitter cup from Him. But the Spirit of God raised up a standard and said, "Lord, if it be Your will, then Your will be done." What dedication He showed to do His Father's will. This example of enduring power means for us as children of God not to give in to our flesh, to please our flesh, but to keep our focus on the Spirit of God as He brings us through the will of God. Be dedicated, a new and anointed soul. Completely dedicated children of God. For God's DNA is in His people.

This book is all about my life, my ups and downs, my ins and outs of how God brought me through all my troubles and trials. Knowing to get to the finish line, I must stay in the race to receive the reward at the end. The many tasks I had to go through to learn how to live in the will of God. No matter how hard the task got, I never gave up. For I believe that God will show me the way out of every hardship. In this book, I learned that God has turned my trials into triumphs. And as Christ died and was resurrected with all power in His hand, I too was totally immersed in His life through baptism, a new life, a new creation to be able to live a deeper love. As you read this book of my life, hopefully, it will give you hope to immerse in God's ways to search for a deeper love in your life. Search deeper for God, the Man, and don't settle for just a man.

Special Thanks

To my children, Antwann Frost and Zy'Atrice Frost.

To all my siblings: Thomas, Toni, Pam, Henry, Kathy, Cynthia, Kim, Jeannie, Greg, Delisa, Angela, Harold, Ronald, Robert, Cietha, Neal, Sheldon, Shannon, Annetta, Karetha, and Phillip.

To my church families: Salem Missionary Baptist Church (thirty-four years); Greater Christian Pentecostal Church, Pastor Sandra

Bryant, Assoc. Pastor Deloris White, and Elder Matthew White (eighteen years); Emmanuel Missionary Baptist Church, Pastor Reginald Frye (eight years); Redemption Christian Tabernacle, Pastor Todd Hoskins (September 2020–).

To my grandchildren: Mykiece, Lyric, Miael, Messiah, Xyon, Mariyah, and my firstborn grandson, Ei'Zayah Frost, who wrote this poem, and I promised I'll put it in my book:

In the Afternoon

Late in the afternoon, I saw the sun going down
The sky wasn't blue late in the afternoon
When you get sleepy, wanting to go to bed late in the afternoon,
You feel a cold chill running through your body late in the afternoon.
Your eyes are getting heavy, and you fall into a deep sleep late in the afternoon,
Where there is peace and quiet, and you feel that you are kept late in the afternoon.
Or is it afternoon?

Introduction

I would like to introduce this book, *Searching for a Deeper Love*, to those who feel as I felt: hurt, mad, broken, depressed, angry, lifeless, alone, lacking commitment, merely existing, without a father, and now without a mother. You should read *Searching for a Deeper Love* so that God's light can shine inside as He molds us into shape on the outside and renew our minds to live and not die. As you read this book, you should begin to feel the love, joy, and peace of heart; the long-suffering as you go through your tasks and trials; meekness, gentleness, and goodness to prepare yourselves not to be tricked by the enemy; and faith and temperance to be strong in the Lord. These nine fruits of the Spirit should always be a part of your lives as you search for a deeper love.

From Now On!

My mother's name was Cloria Mae Lewis. Cain was her maiden name. She was born and raised in Jackson, Mississippi, to her father, Emerson Cain, and her mother, Elizabeth (Bowman) Cain. They left Mississippi in 1945, her mother, father, and her only sister, Mary. They crossed the Mississippi river into Ohio. They had to leave Mississippi because a lady tried to put a hex (witchcraft) on my grandmother to get to her husband. So they left to begin their life in Dayton, Ohio. After being here a little while, Cloria met a man named Buster. A year later, they got married. After he married her, he became so controlling. He didn't want Cloria to leave the house, not even go to church. So he started taking one shoe of every pair she had and hid it so she couldn't go anywhere. Later she found out that he was having an affair with one of the ladies who sang with her in the group the Starlites. She wasn't mad because she wanted a way out of this marriage, and she took it. She left him and the group. She didn't look back. The group couldn't continue to sing because Cloria was the lead singer. She said she wasn't trying to hurt the group, but it seemed like everyone knew about the affair, and nobody, not even her close friends, told her. Well, as time went on, Cloria left Buster, and she progressed in the joy of being in a new state and helping her mother at the restaurant. Then Cloria met a man who thought he was the answer to all women's questions—a smooth talker and a swell dresser. Oh yeah, he caught her attention. But Cloria let him know that she doesn't deal with pimps. He said, "I'm not a pimp. I just look like this, and the ladies love me. My name is Henry, but they call me Big Daddy." Well, after a few dates, Cloria told Henry that their relationship couldn't go any further; he didn't even have a job, and she was not going to take care of a man. Henry said, "No woman takes care of me. I'm my own boss. I do terrazzo. But if you need me to get a nine-to-five job, I can get one tomorrow."

Cloria said, "Well, that's what you got to do." So he did. He started working an eight-hour job and then worked on wooing her until he got her to marry him. In 1951, they had their first child, a little girl. Now, this didn't stop Big Daddy from having his way with other ladies. In 1953, Cloria gave birth to a son, then a daughter in 1954. And then there was me, born in 1956. So here's my story from the beginning, as I remember.

Before there was me, there was him. I was in his mind before I was in my mother's womb. My mom was married to my dad, but I don't know if I was made from love or a fly-by-night feeling. But I would always be searching for that deeper love. My father was not a father to me; that's why I always felt like I needed that father's hug. I would reach in his direction, but I would never receive from him. I wondered if I existed to him, or was my skin tone too dark for him to hug me and call me his little girl? My mom had shown the love that God had placed in her as a mom. But that still didn't touch the void I had for a father's hug. This void had stuck with me all my life, and I would still try and find that love of a father's love. All through my life, I felt shameful because of my dark skin, going to school with shame, and being laughed at because of my nappy hair and my dark skin. I walked with my head down, dealing with the hurt. I wondered why the kids at school were so hateful. Was it because they didn't have a father's love? What was their reason for treating me so badly? As far back as I can remember, I didn't like myself. I would go to school with one pair of shoes for everything, including the gym. I also went to church in the same shoes. My mom said, "When these shoes tear up, then you will get another pair." Wow, these shoes never tore up no matter how I tried to wear them out. The kids at school would talk about me because I would wear these shoes for everything. The other kids would have their gym shoes to change into, but I had those same brown and white Sellocks. I called them Buster Brown shoes. I never did tell my mom how the kids would talk about me from head to toe because my mom always did the best with what she had. I think I was the topic every day. A day didn't go by that my dark skin was not a subject. The kids' talk began to become real inside me. Every time I looked in the mirror, I began to believe what they were saying about me. A dark enemy feeling deep inside, and no one could get to the hurt. I felt rejected, I felt neglected, and I didn't want to go to school. I was angry enough to fight, but my mom wouldn't allow us to fight. So I allowed a lot of the torment to go on.

One of the neighbors, Ms. Brown, who lived across the street from us on Hawthorne Street, told my mom, "You better let those kids fight and take up for themselves. Because we parents aren't going to be around all the time." Her son was one of the bullies in the neighborhood. Ms. Brown said, "Let them kids fight and whop him up." So my mom told us, "If anyone puts their hands on you, then you are to fight back in the name of Jesus."

As time went on and I grew older, there was a little church around the corner on Germantown Street. My mom's group, the Morning Stars, had to sing there. This church had one big drum that a lady put between her legs and played with one large drumstick. They had an old piano in the corner that no one was playing. I asked my mom, "Can I go play?"

The pastor heard me and said, "Sugar, go right over there and make a noise." She didn't know that I knew how to play. I played like never before. I was seven years old, and I felt so free when I played.

After church, a lady asked my mom, "Would it be okay to pick your daughter up for our Sunday school and have her play for our morning services? She is gifted, and she didn't just play the piano. She made a joyful noise. By the way," she added, "my name is Pastor Stallworth, and your daughter will be a blessing to the church." So my mom gave me the okay, and this became my first paying job. I stayed there until Pastor Stallworth passed away. I felt hurt because she believed in me, but now she was gone. I went back to school, and the kids were still being hateful and mean, trying to fight. It got to the point where they started doubling up on us. Not just one family, but three families tried to fight us at one time. We stood our ground: my brother broke his arms, and we kicked butt that day. All the anger I had built up inside was getting some satisfaction.

When we returned to school, they had us in the principal's office. The other families wanted us to be suspended. But it worked in our favor because the principal of Irving School said, "This fight didn't happen during school hours or on school grounds, so I can't suspend them." I smiled. After all was said and done, those families saw that we were not to be messed with. They decided to be our friends.

Going through all this, I wondered, *Why do people have to be so mean?* I had enough going on inside me that didn't feel right. There was something inside me that I was dealing with, and no one was getting to this hurt. As time went on, and I was eleven years old, I started playing for the Salem Baptist Church. Although I enjoyed playing the piano, I still felt a deeper void inside. One thing I learned along this journey is that when a person is hurting, and they begin to move out of that hurt, they either get hurt or they will hurt someone else. As I grew older, I decided I was going to fill this void. I started seeking love even in the wrong places. At the age of thirteen, I joined a church called True Holy, under the leadership of the late Bishop S. L. Henry. I didn't join because of the word he was teaching but because of the boys at the church. They had service on Saturdays, which was their Sabbath day. One Saturday, I stayed all day long. I forgot my mother told me to be at home by 4:00 p.m. to take a family portrait. Well, they were in church so passionately that it captivated me down to the marrow of my bones. I was hypnotized to the point that I didn't want to leave. So it was way past 4:00 p.m., and I knew I was in trouble. I decided to enjoy myself until I got home because I knew I was in big trouble. When I did finally get home, quite naturally, I got a whopping. That was a whopping I would never forget. I decided I would never disobey my mom ever again. That was the last whopping I received from my mom for disobeying her. I didn't want to feel that again. Mom said, "Until you are eighteen years old, you will go to church with me." I was never one to talk back or fuss with my mother, whether she was right or I thought she was wrong in the situation. Whatever Mom said was the truth; I respected my mom like that. I started to watch my two older sisters so I knew what to do and what not to do.

I turned fourteen years old, and my dad decided to let me know about my other brothers and sisters. I was angry at him for the way he treated us. I had made up my mind that I was going to dislike them. But when I met them, it was like the love of God that my mom taught me showed up, and I couldn't do anything but love them. Plus, I wanted to know as much about them as possible. I had anger toward my dad because of how he treated my mom. Time went on, and I entered high school, running track and playing basketball. I spent two years at Roosevelt, then we had to transfer schools because we moved to Colonel White High School. I didn't want to leave Roosevelt. I was a Teddy. My brother, sisters, and cousins were all Teddies, and now, just when I had the chance to be a Teddy, I had to leave and be a Cougar. Still, I had to make the best of this move. So I played basketball and volleyball, and I even ran track. I made it to the state for basketball two years in a row. I was also named MVP in my senior year for music. While I could have graduated during my junior year, I wanted to continue playing ball. My gym teacher, Ms. Doris Black, spoke with the principal, and they let me come back my senior year as a gym aide, and I was still eligible to play ball.

After my senior year, Ms. Black asked me, "What are you going to do next?"

I replied, "I'm not sure."

She said, "If I give you a basketball scholarship, will you go to college?"

I told her I was really through with school. I thought I'd gone as far as I could, but for basketball, I'd consider going. So I ended up attending Central State University, majoring in physical education and music appreciation.

Everything seemed fine for about four months. After the next quarter, some of my classes changed. I had to take a math class and an English class. I asked my counselor, "Do I need math or English for music and PE?"

She responded, "These are required classes for music and PE."

In my English class, the professor instructed the class to read the first four chapters and answer the questions at the end of each chapter. A week later, everyone had turned in their papers. The professor looked up as he graded the papers. He said, "Frost, I didn't see your paper."

I replied, "No, sir, I didn't see the questions after each chapter."

He said, "Everyone else has turned in their answers to the questions," holding up the papers in his hand. "Now I want you to turn to chapter 1. Now go to the end of chapter 1. Now read number 1." I did, and he continued, "Now, answer the question."

I asked, "Where is the question?"

He said, "Are you being funny, Frost? Because you're not."

I replied, "All my life in school, my teachers taught me that a question ends with a question mark. Number 1 ends with a period, which tells me that it's a sentence, not a question."

He asked, "Frost, do you want to be in this class?"

I said, "Honestly, no, I don't."

He said, "You can consider yourself excused."

I replied, "Thank you."

I then began to just goof off, dancing and partying, thinking this class had ruined my chances of my major. I thought if I couldn't pass this class, then I couldn't go any further in college. Every time there was a dance, whether at Central State, Wilberforce, or even in Dayton at the Pookie Pookie Club on college night, I attended. I met Roger Troutman and the Human Body and danced at all their gigs at Wilberforce. Our freshman class had a dance party, and they placed me in charge of getting hotel accommodations for our guest, Ben E. King. So I did my part, and after the dance, while I was giving the hotel details to Mr. King, he said, "Why don't you gather some of your lady friends and let us take you out?" I invited five friends, and we went into town with them. They treated us to a meal and later at the hotel in Xenia. Two of the girls went to Mr. King's room and the drummers' room. The rest of us stayed together in one room eating our food. Later, one of the girls came back to the room and said, "Regina, Mr. King wants you in his room."

I said, "No, he doesn't." And I kept eating.

A few minutes later, Mr. King called up to the room and said, "Tell that b—— I said get down here."

I got up, got my coat, and told the girls, "I'm leaving. Are you coming with me?" They all got up and left with me. We went around to the drummers' room, but the other girl said she was going to stay, so we left. As we were through Xenia from the hotel, an old pickup truck passed us and stopped. The gentleman then asked if we needed a lift. I said, "We need to get back to Central State."

He said, "I can take you all to Route 42," and he did. We walked Route 42 highway back to Central State. It took us about three hours to get back, but we made it. We had so much fun walking we didn't even pay attention to how cold it was. It was a night that I would never forget.

I began to think about what I was going to do about my life's direction. I called my mom and asked if I could come home and work, feeling that I couldn't go any further in school. So that's what I did. I started working at Rike's Department Store in the Salem Mall. I had to take the bus to work. Sometimes I had to walk home because the buses had stopped running before I got off work. Whether it was rain, sleet, or snow, I had to go to work because I promised my mom. My brother Butch was preparing to move out of state and asked me to take over his job playing bass guitar for our father's (Robert Lewis) gospel group, the Clefts of Faith. He said, "I taught you the position so you can do the job when it was time for me to go." They had to audition for the position. They were lined up from the top to the bottom of the basement steps. Father listened to each one, then after they all left, I went to Daddy and told him, "I want to play for you."

He said, "Daughter, you can't play."

I said, "Oh, yes, I can. Butch taught me his position." Daddy let me audition, and I got the job.

Later, in 1976, I landed a better job at Frigidaire, thanks to my sister Kathy, who introduced me to several colleagues. We also joined the company's volleyball and softball teams. What fun we had. Now, see, I would have missed my blessing from her if I had turned my back on her when I met her at fourteen. We don't know who we are going to need in this lifetime, so it pays to just be loving and kind to all, and God will take care of all the rest. My sister and I always had fun working and playing in the games until one fateful volleyball tournament. Only five of our team members showed up. We didn't want to forfeit the game, so we decided to play. We were ahead by five points, and I went up for a spike. But when I came down, another player was under me, causing my knee to turn the wrong way. They called the paramedics. I cried as they moved me off the floor. The referees asked if the team was going to continue to play or forfeit, and they decided to play. But when the paramedics arrived and checked me out, they told me that I needed to go to the hospital. But my team was on the verge of losing the game and the tournament. I told the paramedics I couldn't leave yet. He said, "Ma'am, you can't play on that leg." I hopped back out on the floor, and my team placed me in the middle, rotating around me. The paramedics stood there for a few minutes just to see us play and win the tournament. Then I went to the hospital.

Some people said I was crazy because I could have injured myself more. I replied, "I could have, but I had a determination to finish the race I was in." At the hospital, I found out I had torn all the ligaments in my left knee and needed surgery. The doctor told me that in two years, they would introduce a technology where the surgery would only leave a scar the size of a needle prick. But if I had it now, it would be a baseball-sized scar. I told the doctor I had a lot of patience, but I couldn't wait two years with this painful knee. So I ended up with the baseball scar. Nine weeks after the cast was removed, I was back at work. I also returned to dancing and clubbing after work. I didn't drink or smoke, but I loved dancing the night away. I was good at dancing, so I thought dancing would fill this void deep inside. I would stay out dancing until the early mornings. I had a boyfriend, but that wasn't feeding the hunger and need for that deep void inside. On Saturday nights, I would stay out until five o'clock the next morning. My mother would wake me up at eight o'clock to get ready for church. Everyone staying in Mom's house had to go to church, no questions asked. I played for the church, so I had to be there. Sometimes, after playing for the choir, I would close the piano and sleep. I didn't want to hear the preacher because I felt he was always talking about me. So I thought. Of course, I didn't want to hear anything that would interfere with my fun. I kept searching and looking for love in the wrong places. I listened to different men. They were using those suave words that tickled my ears but didn't have any substance in the words. Different men have different words but the same intentions. They were all up to no good. Only to get what they wanted for the moment. I talked myself into believing that finding a man outside the church would make things better. Guess what, different men talk but have the same results. He got what he wanted and moved on. I wondered why I kept falling for the same lines from men. I continued searching for deeper love. I started visiting my sister Toni in Kansas City, Missouri. In one of my visits, they announced on a radio station that they were having a dance contest with a $100 prize. I told my sister she had to take me there that night, and she did. I couldn't get her to go with me, but she said she'd pick me up when I called her. Being from out of town and not knowing anyone, I scoped out the best male dancers. A shorter man asked me to dance, and I said okay so I could survey who was on the floor, plus I wanted to be seen. Their dancing was different from our dancing in Ohio, so it made me stand out when others were looking at my moves. The short man was so happy to be dancing with me that he asked for a second and a third dance. After the third dance, I excused myself to the ladies' room. When I came out, the short man was headed toward me. I looked toward the exit door and saw a tall man with shoulder-length hair, wearing a wide-brim hat and a superfly suit. I headed over to the tall man before the short man could approach me for a fourth dance.

I asked the tall man, "Sir, can you dance with me so the short man headed this way won't ask me again?"

He laughed, took my hand, and said, "Yes." His voice was so mellow and deep that I melted in his arms as we danced the night away. He didn't let anyone else dance with me for the rest of the night. Except for the $100 contest—I danced with one of Missouri's best. He asked, "Where are you from?"

I told him, "Ohio."

He replied, "Don't tell them. You have to be from Missouri to win."

I responded, "If you don't tell, I won't tell." Of course, I won.

Then the tall man took my hand again and said, "I'm not letting you go." While I was in Missouri, the tall man started calling me and seeing me. Oh, by the way, I found out the tall man's name was Roboam. He was such a gentleman. I returned home to Dayton, we stayed in touch by phone. Our bill was running about $300 to $400 because neither of us wanted to hang up. We talked for days and nights, and I loved the conversations.

Months later, I found out I was pregnant by a man from the church. I cried and stopped talking to Roboam after I told him what happened. The church guy proposed, and I asked him why he wanted to marry me. He replied, "Because you are expecting."

I asked, "So you don't love me?" He didn't answer. I told him that there was no need to make the mistake of marrying if he wasn't committed.

So at the age of twenty-one, I had a son, thinking he would fill the void inside me. I believed he would love me unconditionally. I was scared because I was left to raise a son alone. I really didn't know what I was doing. I had never been in this position before. After my son was born, I began spiraling out of control. I was still playing at the church and dancing at night, searching for love. A year later, I received a call from Kansas City. Yes, it was Roboam. It seemed like we picked back up where we left off with our conversation except we added discussions about my son. After two more years, I invited Roboam to Dayton. A short visit turned into a move-in. Six months later, I was rushed to the hospital, and it was found out that I was expecting my second child. They kept me because I was threatening a miscarriage. After being in the hospital for two days, Roboam was supposed to come and see me. But I haven't heard from him. He didn't know that I was pregnant. He wouldn't answer the call at my godmother's house. She said, "I have been over to your house, and he's not answering the door." So I left the hospital, and when I got home, he was there with a funny look on his face. He seemed shocked I was home, but he didn't even ask how I was doing. He just helped me to the bedroom, and then he said, "I need to go call my mom." Who wants to argue with a man who wants to call his mother? Twenty minutes went by, and thirty minutes went by. After forty-five minutes, I got up out of bed and looked out the window toward my god-mother's apartment, and he was coming out the door. So I went back to the bed. After ten minutes went by, I got up again and looked out the window. I didn't see him, so I went looking around the house. As I opened the closet door, I noticed dirty sheets and towels on the floor. I knew that I had washed before I went into the hospital, and those things had no business being on the floor dirty. As I was headed toward the back door, I thought I heard his laugh next door. So I took a glass, put it up against the wall, and listened. Sure enough, he laughed out again. I put my nightgown on and went and knocked on the next-door neighbor's door. When the lady answered, I said, "Is Roboam in there?" Sure enough, he came out of her bedroom. I said, "You don't know where you stay?" I said, "What are you doing next door? She doesn't even speak to me, but you're in her bedroom?"

He said she offered him a cake. I reminded him that I had baked a cake for him before my hospitalization. Fed up, I told him to call his mother and ask for money to return to Kansas City. He informed me she could send all but fourteen dollars. I replied, "Okay, I've got the rest."

The following day was Thanksgiving and his birthday. We celebrated with family at my mother's house, and I treated him as if nothing had happened, showing him love and warmth. Then when it was time to go home, he thought I had forgiven him for what he had done. But I took him straight to the Greyhound bus station.

He said, "You're still going to send me home?"

I replied, "Oh, yes. I asked two things of you before you came to Dayton: (1) Don't lie to me and (2) don't cheat on me. Everything else can be worked out. But you couldn't keep these two promises. So I'm not mad. You just can't stay with me."

After he was on the bus for about six hours, I called him and told him that I was pregnant. He said, "Can I come back?"

I said, "No, thank you."

He made it home safely, and the calls started every day. He told me he was sorry for the way he treated me, and he promised never to do it again. I told him, "I believe you because you'll never have the chance to do that to me ever again." I finally had a baby girl in July

1981. I received a call that evening. I thought it was Roboam, but it was a woman who said, "I'm his fiancée. I noticed this number all over my bill. He's been calling every day. This is my phone, and he stays in my house. He keeps talking about coming back to Dayton to get his family."

I told her, "I didn't know he didn't have his own. If I were going to take him back, I would have kept him here in Dayton. You don't have to worry about me, but you might have to worry about him because he wants me. You can have him. Also, tell him I had his baby girl, and you all have a nice life together." I hung up the phone and began to cry because I was tired of being hurt. Then I cried out to the Lord because I was tired of being played by men, tired of trying to make it work. Here I was again, raising another child by myself. I wanted a son and a daughter but not like this. The choices I made for temporary pleasure, just to please men, caused me hurt and stress. I decided, after I got through crying, I was ready to grow up. I would not let men hurt me again. It's up to me what I allow into my life. I told the Lord I was ready to live solely for Him.

The Lord's voice spoke to me and said, "I told you to love Me first. For I will never leave you nor forsake you." I told the Lord that I believed Him, and I was committing my life completely to Him. Now I was ready to live. Even my children, I give them back to Him. I need Him to help me to survive.

A month after I had my daughter, I sat in a revival service with my aunt Mary from Atlanta, Georgia. Amid her sermon, she pointed me out and said, "The Lord said He heard your cry. You're tired of living like you do, and you want to give yourself completely over to the Lord."

I said, "Yes!" with my baby in one hand and the other hand stretched out to the Lord. As I walked toward her, she told me that God loved me, and that I had to stop searching for a man and start seeking the Man.

"The Man will love and keep you. He will never leave you. He's been waiting for you to get into position." My mom took my baby as I walked toward the front of the church. My aunt Mary said, "When I touch you, you will speak in an unknown tongue. It might seem strange, but it's a language between you and God. Don't be dismayed. As you confess with your mouth and believe in your heart, He will forgive and save you. Do not be afraid anymore of the direction you're going in because the Lord is with you. As you acknowledge Him in all your ways, He will direct your path." She said, "Take heed to these words for they are instructions from the Lord." When she touched me, it happened just as she said.

When I left that night, I felt so renewed. My life seemed to have started over like I was a newborn, but I was twenty-four years old. I felt cleansed. All my sins had been forgiven. I no longer felt bound. My aunt said, "Since you believe in Jesus's life, burial, and resurrection, and you confess with your mouth that Jesus Christ is your Lord and Savior, you are without a doubt saved. Don't let anyone tell you differently. But now you must sanctify yourself, which means setting yourself apart from the ways of this world."

I said, "This sounds easier said than done."

She said, "It's easier when you live as Jesus instructed." It then hit me that God had let me feel something good inside. I felt changed. I was able to feel a newness.

After my daughter turned one year old, my sister Cynthia came and asked me to help her with a vision that the Lord gave her. I accepted although I was still singing with the Morning Stars along with my mom. So the group was formed with a mother and three daughters. We started rehearsing, and the Lord gave my sister the name Heavens Unlimited. I turned my resignation in with the Morning Stars so I could give Heavens Unlimited my full attention. Weeks went by, and Mom was still going to rehearsals with the Stars. Of course, she had been with this group for thirty-four years, singing lead. But the Lord told her to move, and she did. She moved on with Heaven's Unlimited. Mom said, "Baby, we are not going to understand everything God tells us to do or say, but just be obedient to His Word, and God will take care of the rest. Everything has a season, and when it's your season, you are to walk in it." My sister Cynthia and I started writing songs as the Lord was giving them to us for Heaven's Unlimited. All my songs were about my life. I got to thinking about the Lord and how he saved my life. He raised me up from a fornicating life.

Now just because I decided to accept the Lord as my Savior didn't mean that the enemy was going to leave me alone. The closer I was getting to God by reading His Word to live His Word, the more tasks the enemy plotted against me, hoping that I would fall. Well, I wish that I could tell you that I would never fall again since I have accepted Christ, but that would be lying. The truth of the matter is I fell time and time again. The Lord let me know, "For this, I went on the cross to redeem you to Me. The cross has no power, but the power lies in the blood that I shed for you. My daughter, I forbid you to sin. But if you do, you have an advocate that stands in the gap for you. You have an intercessor, so you don't have to stay in your sins. So get up again, let Jesus dust you off, and come back to Me, for I'm married to the backslider."

As time went on, I spent quality time with God's Word and with Heaven's Unlimited, writing songs and trying to fill this inner void. Yes, I was still looking for that father's love. In 1986, I ended up marrying my stepfather's nephew from Memphis, Tennessee (I know, go figure). My stepfather was a good man, and I didn't call him stepfather. He was my father. He married my mom with nine children that were not his by blood. He went against what his family thought, and he went toward the love of my mom. Well, his nephew J. T. came to live in Dayton with him. I thought if he was a Lewis, he might be like his uncle. After about seven months of being around J. T., he started spending time with me and the children. When I had to sing, he would help me with my equipment. He was all right with whatever I had to do. Eventually, I married him. I was still trying to fill my father's love inside me. No matter who loved me, it was not going deep enough to fill that void. About fourteen months after the marriage, the real person came out. He changed; he wasn't nice anymore. He would get up at 5:00 a.m. every day and be gone by 6:00 a.m. He didn't work at this time. I didn't know, but I found out he was leaving to go smoke weed. He became so dominant in the marriage to the point he didn't want me to leave the house. He would check my mileage in my car from home to church. He would ask many questions like, "Who did you hug today? 'Cause I know your family is known for hugging and kissing." I told him my mom taught us to greet like that. He stopped helping me with anything dealing with the church. And when things didn't go his way, my house was not a home.

Three years had passed, and the Lord had really been working in me. I finally accepted my calling into the ministry. My husband was not happy. He said, "I don't want no preacher for a wife." He would fuss and cuss, even though I didn't fuss or cuss with him. This made him more angry. As the Lord began talking to me and working with me, my life began to change. The Lord had me on a seven-week walk. I walked with a sign around my neck that said, "If you want to know about the goodness of Jesus, shake my hand." The Lord had given me instructions not to talk on this journey unless someone shook my hand. I was questionable about this walk at first because when this word came into my mind, it was in the month of February, cold and snowy.

So I said, "Lord, is this really You telling me to go out in the cold to shake hands?"

And the voice spoke to me and said, "I take the foolish things of the world to confound the wise."

I said, "Okay, Lord, does this mean go, or don't listen to that voice?" I decided to listen and be obedient because I do know that the enemy is not going to tell you to go speak on the goodness of Jesus. While on this walk, I met many souls who were in need of a friend.

I had one person pass me up on Germantown Street. He was driving a white Cadillac car. He stopped, backed up, and got out of his car. He came over and shook my hand and said, "Now tell me something."

And I began to tell him how Jesus loves him. And Jesus lived and died for him. And after three days and three nights, Jesus rose with all power in his hand. "And because He rose, you can rise above any situation in your life because He gave you power to trample over the enemy. You don't have to bow down and accept the enemy in your way. Use the power that Jesus has given you and live." The man shook my hand even harder.

He said, "Thank you. You just saved my life because I was getting ready to go and commit suicide." His eyes filled up with tears as he thanked me again. I told him we give all praises and glory to our Father God for He is watching over our souls. The man said, "I gave my soul to him a long time ago, but I was just fed up with this life."

I told him, "If you work the Word of God, then God's Word will work for you. His word works on our good days as well as your bad days, for He reigns on the just and the unjust, with no respect for people. He said to cast your cares on Him if you can't handle it. There are certain things He wants us to do, but if those things in your life get too heavy, Jesus said He will bear it for us."

The man let go of my hand and kept saying, "Thank You, Jesus." He got in his car and took off.

I said, "Wow, Lord, you are a miracle worker!"

When I got home, I wanted to tell someone what happened. I began to talk to my husband and he said, "I don't want to hear anything about your walk." He was so mean and angry that Christ was using me. One day, his mother, brothers, and sister came to visit. He went to work, but I had to wait for him to call me to pick him up from work.

It was past 6:00 p.m., and he hadn't called. His mom and I started dinner, and then at about eight, the door opened up, and it was him. He went to the kitchen and hollered at me and said, "Let me see you upstairs."

I thought, *Oh, Lord, what has happened now?* When I got to my room, he closed the door and blocked it so I wouldn't leave. I had a round bed with a white heart-shaped fur backboard. He started cursing at me. He was talking so fast I could only catch every other word, so he wasn't making any sense. "You've got to calm down so I can understand you."

He said, "From now on, that car is going with me."

I said, "That's not happening. It's my car."

He said, "Why didn't you answer the phone?" I told him the phone hadn't rung all day. He started cursing at me again. I didn't want to stay in the room so I got up to leave. He grabbed me and ran around the bed as he chased me. I then jumped across the bed to get to the door, and he caught me and slammed the door closed. He grabbed me by my neck and began choking me. I began to see my life go before me, and everything went dark. I was about to black out. The only thing I could do was scratch his face. His brother and my son came into the room and got him off of me.

My son said, "I'm going to kill you."

I said, "No, son, you will not sit in jail for my foolishness. I'll handle this. He will be dealt with."

I called the police. They sent two policewomen. They spoke to us separately. A policewoman told me, "If he wants to press charges on you, he can because we see the marks on his face caused by you, but there are no marks on you."

I said, "It's because he was choking me, and the only thing I could do was scratch his face." So I told her, "If you couldn't get him to leave, then you policemen can go, and I'll handle this myself." As they were leaving, I went crazy praising the Lord in my house. Every day, every night. His family also left to go back home.

The following Saturday, I went to rehearsal, and when I returned, my house was cleaned out. Plus, he took my car. Mind you, this man came to Dayton with just a suitcase. But he took everything out of my house: my living room, dining room, three-bedroom beds, and dressers. My children's clothes were all on the floor, where he took them out of their dressers. I was hurt, but not for me, but for my children. I asked my children to forgive me for putting them in this situation. As we tried to pull the house back together and settle down for the night, the Lord let me know not to be angry anymore, but to look at this as a blessing.

"For you need this space for the new furniture coming in that God has in store for you. Also, remember when I said, 'You reap what you sow.' You remember you helped clean out a house, now someone cleaned out yours, so don't be angry. I have strengthened you to go through this struggle."

I got a call from him weeks later; his mom told him his niece was playing on the phone and turned the ringer off. Well, I said, she did me a favor. "I'm glad you found out. I told him he should be receiving a package real soon because I have filed for divorce."

He said, "Can we try again?"

I said, "No, I'm done."

As time went on, I was seeking the Lord to teach me how to love myself. Because I have been hurt so much by men, I didn't want to be bothered by men. God said, "Let Me love you and show you how to love yourself." So when it was time for me to go to court, my ex-husband, J. T., brought a lady with him from Memphis. I don't know what that was supposed to mean, but I didn't feel angry, upset, or anything. That let me know I was over him.

The judge asked me, "Ms. Lewis, what do you want out of this divorce?"

I said, "Nothing." She said, "Ms. Lewis, you said that your husband took your car along with other items from your home, and you don't want anything?"

I said, "I don't want anything."

She asked me, "Why not?"

I told her, "I don't want him to think he helped me get back up on my feet, so I don't want anything from this man."

She said, "So be it," and she granted me my divorce. I felt so relieved I was able to breathe again. About two or three months later, he contacted my brother, trying to get in contact with me. My brother laughed. I thought he was joking. He said, "I'm for real."

So I called him. I said, "What's going on? Is your mother all right?"

He said, "Oh yeah, she's fine."

So I asked, "What did you need me to call for?" He said he just wanted to hear my voice and see how I was doing. I told him, "I'm fine, and don't worry about me. I'm highly favored." He didn't know what that meant, but that was okay because I knew. The Lord has blessed me to come out of that wilderness.

Ten years after my first marriage, I ran into a high school friend that I had a crush on. He was a truck driver. I introduced him to my mother, which meant I really liked him. He was the one to give me a nickname in high school ("Crazy Legs") because I was bow-legged, knock-kneed, and pigeon-toed. (I know. Go figure.)

We went out a couple of times. He finally asked me, "Is it true we can't go to bed unless we are married?"

I said, "Yes, that's true."

Well, his visits got shorter and shorter until there were no visits.

So I said, "Okay, I understand what his motive was." What I learned from this is this: Just because it looks good to you doesn't mean it's good for you.

Time went on, and I ran into another old friend. I would never let him know that I liked him back in the day because my mom had instilled a fear in me that I better not look at a boy. Well, this friend started coming around more and more, and I began to feel those old feelings I had for him back in the day. And the spirit of God began to let me know that he was going to be my husband. But I was to wait and stay strong in the Lord.

Time went on, and he started pressing me to listen to the call of my flesh. The enemy was telling me to listen to the call of my flesh. The enemy was telling me, "You don't have to wait. God had already told you this man was going to be your husband, so why wait? Go for it so you can please God and flesh all at the same time." Do you know I listened to that spirit? I thought it was the right spirit, but how wrong I was.

I thought I could help the Lord and speed up the process of waiting since He said he was to be my husband, and he was a good man, and my steps are ordered by the Lord. I told him the only way I could indulge in my flesh was to be married. So he said, "Let's do it."

Now mind you, I haven't seen this man in twenty years. I didn't know what he was involved in or what he was doing. I knew back in the day he was in church, but I didn't know if he was still following Christ or not. I was just trying to fix this so I could please my flesh and God too. Sometimes we think we're doing it God's way, and God is saying,

> If my people which are called by my name would
> humble themselves and pray and seek my face

turn from their wicked ways, then will I hear from heaven, I'll forgive their sins, and I'll heal their land. (2 Chronicles 7:14)

I don't know why we think God, who is omnipresent (He's everywhere at the same time) beholding all evil and the good, and who is omnipotent (He has all power in His hand), needs help from us to fix something. The only thing I was thinking about was my flesh and to stay right with God. But God was not pleased with my help. Well, I was too blind to see that the old man had woken up inside me, and I was not trying to shut him down. So I finally married this man, and I had convinced myself and others that God had organized this.

Two weeks after the marriage, he didn't come home one Friday after he got paid. He was a professional drywall finisher. I've seen the before and after projects of his work. He is awesome at what he does. He had many clients. Jobs were lined up, but I didn't know what happened for him not to come home. His mom and family were not telling me anything. Finally, he came in on Monday. He didn't look right or smell right. I began to question what was going on, but he wouldn't answer the questions. This went on weekend after weekend, and after three months of this pattern, I found out that he was on drugs. I was so sick to my stomach because I allowed this situation into my life. He was a good guy to go to work, but he was working to support his habit and not his family.

I went through many obstacles with this marriage. If I would lock him out, he would break into my house. I would call the police, and I would tell them that he is not wanted here. The police said, "He can break in a door or window and not be charged."

I said, "Okay, you all can go. I'll handle this myself." I thought, *How did I get back to this wilderness again?* I said, "Lord, I got married so my bed won't be defiled."

The Lord said (in an angry voice), "*I told you to wait* and to stay in Me! You were so busy trying to please yourself that you messed up the blessing. Yes, this man was to be your husband, but there was a waiting period. He needed some adjustments in his life to be able to deal with a woman of God. And you needed some adjustments in your life to be able to accept one of My kings. Yes, you didn't see the king in him. You just saw the shell of the man. But because you rushed and did it your way, this is the result of your actions." The Spirit said, "What you should learn from this experience is to acknowledge God in all your ways so that you won't keep doing the dumb stuff, even when it comes to your relationships. Let God be your man. Let God love you, and let God teach you to love Him with all thine heart, mind, and soul. For He is a jealous God. You are to keep Him first in your life, and He will love you as He loves the church. God will never hurt you. He'll never leave you, nor will He forsake you." The Spirit said to me, "I want to teach you to be a virtuous woman."

After five years of this marriage, I got my divorce. I thought I had learned my lesson about moving too swiftly and too soon. I know I heard God's voice that told me this was my husband, and I also heard the enemy's voice that said, "You don't have to wait." But the choice was mine. If we don't know the difference in the voices, we will always fall for the wrong voice.

God said, "My people know My voice." Now when you know the difference in the voices and still choose to follow the wrong one, you will go through a wilderness. You will be whipped with many stripes from the Lord because you know what's right but choose to do the wrong. It is best to do anything or everything in God's way, no matter how long you have to wait. The short way is not always the better way. I then asked the Lord to forgive me. Yes, I repented because I sinned. I went against God's way.

"I need You, Lord, to teach me Your ways and Your statutes so that I may not err against You."

He told me to put on the whole armor of God. "You're not dressed properly. And when you get dressed, I want you to stay dressed with the helmet of salvation. Put on the breastplate of righteousness and the shield of faith, wherewith you shall be able to quench all the fiery darts of the wicked. Have your loins girt about with truth. Also, the sword of the Spirit, which is the Word of God. You are to have your feet shod with the preparation of the gospel of peace. Then pray always with all prayer and supplication in the spirit, and watch with all perseverance and supplication for all saints."

You must stay dressed so you will recognize the enemy when he shows up. Oh yes, he is going to show up. But you are on guard at all times, even while you are asleep. Pray so that an angel watches over your spirit while the body rests. And as the Lord began to teach me his statutes, every part of me said, "Yes to His ways, and yes to His will." The enemy looks at me now, and I can recognize him approaching. I'm able to rebuke him as he approaches instead of running away. The enemy is out seeking whom he may devour. Whoever would allow him to come in and be used. But it's too late for him with me. He should have killed me when he had the chance, but now I know my redeemer lives, and He is with me. My redeemer knows my present and my future. He knows my beginning and my ending. The enemy thought he had me. He tried to kill me, but I escaped, and now he can't touch my soul because it belongs to the Lord.

God's Word said, "All who have accepted Jesus, My Son, I place them in His hand. He shall not lose one." So I abide in Jesus, and His word abides in me, and I believe that anything I ask, He will supply according to His righteousness. The enemy knows that once we accept Jesus as our Lord and Savior, we shall receive power after the Holy Ghost has come upon us. We become soldiers in the army of the Lord, armed and dangerous. Why? Because the enemy's job is to kill, steal, and destroy. But my cry is to God's people, to all who have accepted Jesus as their Lord and Savior, and also those who haven't yet. Listen: Earth is not an everlasting place. There is a new heaven and a new earth. And there is also hell. Before you leave this place called Earth, you must choose this day whom you will serve: either Jesus or Satan, the enemy. Satan seeks you out to devour you because he knows how powerful you can become if you stay with God. The enemy aims to claim more souls than God. His entire motive is to outdo God. That's why he was cast out of heaven. A beautiful angel, but jealousy made him greedy, and he desired more recognition than God. Thus, God cast him and a third of the angels that followed him out of heaven. Since then, he has been recruiting souls to join him in an eternal lake of fire.

As time went on, in 1999, I had to see a doctor for a pinched nerve. When the doctor took the X-ray to see what needed to be done, he noticed that I required a bone fusion immediately. He asked, "How did you hurt your neck?" I replied that I had worked at a company called Sugar Creek Packing in 1991. We were packing thirty-pound boxes of bacon. I was transferring the boxes from the track to the skid, four boxes wide and eight boxes deep. Later, they switched to forty-pound boxes. When I reached the seventh level, something in my elbow snapped, and pain shot up to my neck. I endured the pain for the rest of the day but visited the hospital the next day. I kept telling the doctors that something was wrong with my neck.

A year after the injury, they decided to operate only on my elbow, leaving my neck untreated. From 1991 to 1999, I suffered from this pain for eight years. Finally, someone identified the problem. I underwent surgery, where they took a bone from my hip and inserted it into my neck. Three days post-surgery, I was sent home, but I found it difficult to swallow. The soreness got worse as the night progressed. My dad said, "Why would they send you home in this state? You should be in the hospital." So my daughter took me back, where they discovered an infection in my neck. The doctor who did the surgery was very mean and upset that I came back. He decided to pick the infection out while I was woken up in the emergency room. I was hollering in pain, and my daughter intervened and told the doctor to sedate me, and put me to sleep. So they did.

After a five-day hospital stay, I went to my parents' house to recover. My bed was set up downstairs in the dining room. Each day around 6:00 a.m., my father would read the Bible aloud. Sometimes his reading would wake me up because he would be trying to pronounce certain words and he needed help. So I would wake up and read with him. We had never done this before. My father couldn't read, but he would always get the Bible and read it every morning and every evening. As I was healing, my father and I bonded ever so close. He told me as he sipped his coffee, "Daughter, you will be a great preacher if you read the Word every morning and evening." Once I got well enough to return home, we started giving scriptures to each other that we had to search and study in the Bible each week. This was fun. I learned I needed this in my life. More than ever because the enemy was after me. And I really didn't know how much until I started reading and learning about God. The Lord put in my spirit to stay dressed up to be able to stand against the wiles of the devil. I questioned, "Lord, I've accepted You as my Savior, so why is the enemy coming after me?"

He replied, "Since you've dedicated your soul to Me, he is going to try to devour you every chance he gets. He is out seeking whomever will allow him to come in. This is why you must stay dressed up in the armor: love, joy, peace, long-suffering, meekness, goodness, gentleness, kindness, and temperance. These should reside in your mind, heart, emotions, and soul." The enemy wants to trap you, trick you, and trip you up to steal from you every blessing that God has instore for you. He wants to destroy your mind that is in Christ Jesus and to kill you by putting fear into your mind and heart. But God said, "I don't give my people the spirit of fear. But of power and of love and of a sound mind" (1 Timothy 1:7).

I'm learning we are to fear the Lord which means to respect God's Word and to be obedient to God's Word. I began to write song after song all about the up and down obstacles of my life. I wondered why it was so hard to find the love that I needed to live. I got more into the word seeking the Lord hoping to find an answer. The more I read, the more He let me know that He would be my man. He promised that He wouldn't leave me nor forsake me. He would always be by my side. He called me *friend*. And He let me know a friend doesn't mean He knows me for a long time, but a friend is one that never will leave you, for a friend loveth at all times. He promised to love me as He does the church, never causing it harm. I remember talking to the Lord one day, and I told Him that all through my life, I have been blessed. I've always had a roof over my head, and my mom always ensured we had food to eat. I've always had clothes on my back. Maybe not the name brand, but no matter whose name was on the label, we were clean and neat. My mom introduced me to God at an early age. So by the age of forty-four, I truly understood about God supplying all my needs. For instance, a memory from when I was in need: I was preparing for my twenty-fifth class reunion at Colonel White High School. On the first night, I attended the opening, and it was wonderful to see everyone there. However, I was scared to go because I was by myself. I could have invited my ex-husband to go with me. He would have been happy to go, but I didn't want to use him like that for it would have been a show-off, and he probably would have thought we were getting back together. I don't like using people for my satisfaction, so I went by myself. It was good to hear the success in everyone's life. They were amazed that I was a minister. When asked if I still danced, I replied, "Yes, I just changed partners." As I left that night, I noticed all the good-looking cars. No one had a bad-looking car except me. When I got home, I told my children about my night, and they were happy for me.

The next day, I started getting prepared for the banquet and dance. When I got ready to leave, I went outside, and my son was finishing up washing my car. It was shining. I said, "Thanks, and I love you for doing this for Mom."

He said, "Enjoy yourself, Mom. You deserve it." Well, about the time I pulled up to the banquet hall and parked the car, I noticed a little speck on the hood of the car. So when I got out, I looked a little closer and noticed there were bugs all over the car. It looked like every bug I came in contact with was stuck in my car. I called my son and told him what was happening, and I asked him what he did to the car because everything was sticking to the car.

He said, "Mom, you told us how everybody had nice, pretty cars, so I wanted you to have a nice clean car, so I washed it, then I greased it down with Vaseline to make it shine." I laughed so hard till I cried. But I told my son, "You are the best son, and God gave you to me. I thank God for this gift." So I went in, and I had a good time, but I left before anyone would come out to see a Vaseline-greased car with bugs. This wasn't a big need, but it just showed how God will show up for His people no matter how little or how big the need is.

I believe God's word when He said, "I will supply all your needs according to my riches in glory.

I spoke to God and said, "I believe Your Word, but I've never had a one-on-one encounter with You. But whatever was needed was provided for us."

Two months later, Heaven's Unlimited was preparing to go to Laurel, Mississippi, to sing at the Holy Spiritualaires Anniversary. Around noon on Friday, I had to pick up my daughter and grandson from the Children's Hospital. As we approached downtown, I stopped at the signal light and heard the Lord say to me three times, "I'll never leave you nor forsake you." After the third time, I heard a different voice that said, "I gotcha." The next thing I remember is sitting on the side of the car, on the ground, with my grandson, Izayah. I could hear voices, but I couldn't understand what they were saying. I couldn't move my legs. When I tried to get up, my legs wouldn't move. I couldn't even feel them. Eventually, a policeman approached, reaching for my grandson, and I released him from my arms. My daughter took the baby from the policeman. They took me to the hospital.

I asked my daughter what happened, and she said, "Just let them check you." I couldn't feel anything from the waist down.

A doctor came in to check me out, then left, only to return with a long needle. He pricked my feet, but I felt nothing. He told the policeman, "If she was faking, that would have shown it. No human can endure that kind of poke in the feet and not react."

I asked, "Am I paralyzed?" My family surrounded me. I was so scared. They cleared the room and began doing tests and X-rays to determine what was going on, but all the tests returned normal. They moved me to a room, and I asked again, "What had happened? Can anybody tell me why I can't feel my legs?"

My daughter told me, "Mom, just rest, and we'll be back."

As I closed my eyes, I questioned God. "I've served in church all my life, playing the piano. I could have played for the world, but I played for You, Lord. Why have You taken my ability to walk?"

Then in the midst of a white cloud, I heard a voice that spoke out and said, "Silence! You were busy with your business and not My Father's business. Stop complaining. I want you to hear from God.

You're not doing Me a favor going to church. I want you to be the church. I want you to know My presence."

I said, "Couldn't You show me in another way?"

The voice said, "I came to you many times, but you wouldn't listen. And another way could be a worse way than this. I want you to take heed of what I'm saying to you. You were looking at the messengers instead of listening to the message that I sent you. If you love Me, then love My people. If you love Me, then you keep My commandments. Now this is your one-on-one encounter. I had to get your attention because you were headed for a great fall." The voice continued, "I didn't raise Lazarus from the grave because I could, but I did it because there was some unbelief standing around. As I called Lazarus forth, he came, but he was still bound by the wraps they had him wrapped in. So Jesus gave the word to free him, release him, and let him go. Then he was free. So you may be alive but bound with the cares of the world. You may not be behind jail bars, but your mind is being locked up. So I say to you, release and let go. Let God free you from yourself and others." God said, "You know My name, but you don't know who I am. So I'm allowing this to happen because there is some unbelief standing around you that needs to see that I'm God. And besides Me, there is no other God. But I want you to believe without seeing. Don't go by what your situation looks like. For the greatness of your obstacle is for the greatness of God's opportunity to show up for you. Just as God had shown up for His Son Jesus in His suffering, He will also show up for you. So hold on to your faith in believing and knowing God. The great I Am. No matter what your stumbling block, barrier, hurdle, obstruction, hindrance, snag, drawback, handicap, complications, difficulty, problems, or disadvantage, and if you can't find yourself in one of these, just know and believe—whatever you are dealing with in your life, by faith in God, you can overcome any obstacle."

The voice said to me, "I want you to tell My people I'm soon to come. No man knows the day nor the hour when the Son of God shall appear. Many won't believe you, but you don't have to prove yourself. Many will guess and wonder. But no matter how prestigious their title, it does not make them the author and finisher of your faith. Remember this: God's Word shall accomplish what it sets out to do. For God's Word does not lie. It will not return to Me void. Tell my people to heed My word. Be prepared to meet the King. Whatever you know that is not right with God, rectify it so you can meet your bridegroom in peace. You don't need a psychic, palm reader, or a false prophet to tell you what to correct."

Jesus said, "Seek Him first while He may be found. I'm not lost, for I have chosen you. So now receive Me and stay in position to inherit eternal life. If you knock, the door will be opened to you. As you seek Me, My love, My peace, My ways, and My statutes, the kingdom of glory will manifest powerfully. Prepare yourself, My child, for I am about to open the sky for the second coming. Some didn't believe me when I told Noah to build an ark because it was going to rain for forty days and forty nights. It might have sounded strange to them, but it happened. Understand that there will be skeptics around you doubting this, but stand firm in the truth and let God's light shine through you. Those who don't believe My word will experience My wrath. I now name you Queen Re' (Queen Ray). I will raise you again as a bold soldier to love My people."

I said, "Lord, You know how they talk about me and slander me."

He replied, "They did it to Me first, so because you are a part of Me, you'll endure similar trials. But you are to know Me through the suffering, then you will reign with Me if you faint not along the way. Queen Re', keep your focus on Me. No matter what happens, turn to the Word to bring you out. Just as Peter walked out on the waters when I bid him to come unto Me, he took his focus off Me and began to sink. If you lose focus on Me, you will go down. So keep your mind, eyes, ears, tongue, body, and emotions focused on Christ. And He will take care of the rest. You see, Queen Re', I didn't bring you to this bridge to fall without showing you a way out if or when you fell. I wanted you to know that no matter how high the bridge is over troubled waters, I am still God, ready to carry you over that troubled bridge. If I brought you to this, I can and will carry you through this. No matter what the situation looks like, just keep your focus on Me."

The Spirit of God told me to get off the medicines. He said, "The medicines are killing you." He continued, "I was bruised for you. I was bruised for your iniquities. I was bruised for your transgressions. And by My stripes that I took for you, believe this: you are healed. Just believe My word without seeing the manifestation. Queen Re', I'm not testing you because I already know what you will do. But your faith is being tried. I gave you the power to withstand the wiles of the enemy. So come off the medicines."

Then I woke up. I don't know how long I was out. I saw a nurse go past my room. She said, "You're back with us."

I asked, "What happened?"

I then saw my daughter in the corner chair, and as she got up, she said, "Mom, we had an accident." She explained that she was calling my name when the light changed, but I just kept on driving through the next light.

I asked, "Did I hurt anyone?"

She replied, "Yourself."

I said, "I can't feel my legs."

The nurse remarked, "For a couple of nights, you've been talking out of your head, and you weren't making any sense." But to me, I was making plenty of sense because I was talking to God. I told the nurse that I couldn't take any more medicine.

She left, and then a doctor came in. He asked, "Ms. Lewis, what's going on?"

I replied, "The Lord told me to come off the medicines because they are killing me. I've been on oxycontin for thirteen months."

He said, "Well, we can't just stop the medicines like that. You have to be weaned off."

I said, "The Spirit of God told me to stop."

He inquired, "So are you refusing medications?"

I replied, "Yes, just find out why I'm not walking, please."

The doctor said, "Ms. Lewis, I won't fight against your religion and beliefs, but just as long as you know, the choice is yours."

I responded, "I don't have a religion, but I do have a relationship with God, so I must follow what God said to do, but I do thank you."

The doctor said, "We will find out how and why you became paralyzed."

After being in Grandview Hospital for a week, I began to see people with one leg and people with no legs, but I still had my legs. So I began to be thankful. I was still a little angry because I couldn't move my legs. I couldn't feel anything in my legs, but I still had them. Something came over me, and I started thanking God. Once I finally found out what this test was all about, and that the Lord was showing me where I was headed because I was living for myself and pleasing myself, He let me see I was hell-bound. If I wanted eternal life with Christ, I must live this life completely in Him. Yes, being a light for Him to show those walking in darkness that Jesus is the way out of your misery and strife. For God has an eye in every place, seeing the good and the evil. He sees everything we do. We can't hide from God. I was sneaking and hiding from people, doing wrong, but God saw my good and my bad. Just because the good outweighs the bad doesn't mean that God will let you get by. There are consequences for our actions. Whether good or bad, we are still going to pay for the deeds done in this body. Now He was giving me another chance to get it right with Him. He said, "Queen Re', you either get right while only you and I know it, or I make you an open book, and they'll all read you. You either get right with God, or you will get left by God at the second coming of Jesus Christ."

As I went into the second week in the hospital, they had me in therapy. I started talking to the therapist in such a positive way. She asked, "Can you feel anything in your legs?"

I replied, "No, ma'am."

She said, "But the way you're talking, it sounds like you already can walk."

I told her, "Yes, I'm walking already. I believe it without seeing it."

She asked, "So you're walking in the spirit?"

I said, "That's it."

I then started talking to other patients to encourage them that God loves us and that our circumstances do not determine our end of the road. We are to believe that He is greater than the storm in our lives and that He is our protector. There was a gentleman who had lost both legs. He stated, "You can be happy, but I lost out."

I told him, "You might not have your legs right now, but you still have life. Don't look at the small package but look at the blessing of life. Now it's what you do with the rest of your life. It's not how you started this race, but it is about how you end the race. I'm here to tell you to go all the way across the finishing line, and at the end of your finishing line, God has another pair of legs for you. Just don't give up on God. In every situation, there is a reason for the results. Sometimes we use the wrong tools of life and get a bad result. Sometimes we use the right tools and get a result we don't understand. But in every situation, we are to learn from that experience. Everything in this life is going to cease, but your soul will live an eternal life. Either in the new heavens if you accept Jesus as your Lord and Savior, and you must live completely in Him, or in hell where you will have your place in the lake of fire with Satan. Just know, sir, I would rather enter the new heavens with half of a body than enter hell with a whole body. So I'm telling you we must choose this day whom we are going to serve. The most important thing in life is that our soul is returned to the one that gave us life. And that is Jesus Christ." I told him I would rather accept the Lord now and find out at the end that there is no God than not accept the Lord Jesus as my Savior and then find out at the end that He is real and it's too late for me because I didn't accept Him in my life. So while you still have breath in your body, take the opportunity to choose Jesus and let His Word work for you as you let His Word work in you. I told him a lot of our situations in our life are happening because of the choices we made or didn't make in our life. Accepting the Lord in your life doesn't mean that your life is going to go as smoothly as butter, but it means God's Word will help you and direct you in every area of your life.

He said, "I can't walk again."

I replied, "Yes, you can. I have my legs, but I'm paralyzed. But I'm walking in the spirit of God. I believe His Word when He promised me that I would walk again if I would just believe without seeing it. Just use what you got for the Lord, and He'll take care of the rest."

He said, "Thanks for talking to me."

I then went to my room to get ready for bed. I felt so happy and still couldn't feel anything in my legs.

As the night drew late, the Lord started showing me dreams, and when I would tell the person in the dream, something began to happen. The first dream was about my brother, D. He was going to take four ladies to teach them to sing. They went to the church, but they could not sing. My brother and his wife were sitting on a couch, and these ladies were standing on the right side of the couch. But when he stood up, a line appeared between him and his wife. I approached him and told him the Lord said, "There is free government money you can get that you don't have to pay back to start your business. But you must stay with your wife to receive it. You shouldn't leave with those ladies because they can't sing, which means that relationship is not about singing."

When I woke up, I called my brother and asked him to come and see me. He came, and he brought his wife along. I told him about the dream, and he said, "I know that had to be of the Lord to show you this because we're on our way to Cincinnati, Ohio, right now for a meeting on free money from the government. Plus, I hadn't told anyone that my wife and I had decided to split."

I told him, "You got your answer. If you want the money, then don't leave your wife. Do it like the Lord said." Suddenly, I felt something in my big toe—a tingling sensation. It was a minor feeling, but I did feel it.

The second dream I had was about my cousin Jeannie. I was looking for my cousin to let her know that the family dinner was going to be at my place, which turned out to be a big party boat. I went to her job where she was a correctional officer. I saw this big yellow bus full of inmates. I got on the bus looking for Jeannie. As I started down the aisles calling her name, I felt great fear. The farther I walked to the back of the bus, the more fear I felt. As I turned around, I asked, "Does anyone know where Jeannie is?" When I reached the front of the bus, her brother H. G. was sitting in the driver's seat. I asked him, "Have you talked to Jeannie?"

He said, "She had to leave the company because it got too stressful, so she went to get a drink." I told him Jeannie didn't drink. I then got off the bus and headed down the street.

Jeannie pulled up in a red car, and I said, "What are you doing drinking and driving? I'll drive you to the family dinner." But when I attempted to grab the door handle, she took off and sideswiped a young man's car. They started shooting at her as they sped off. I decided to go back to the party boat to tell Mom that Jeannie was on the run. When I got back, my sister Toni was holding a baby that belonged to my daughter Z, but she was too young to have this child. So I told my sister I'll take care of the baby until Z is able to.

I went to find Mom to let her know about Jeannie. I found Mom on the upper deck, and she said, "I'm trying to find Cynthia. Will you help me?"

I said, "Yes, Mom."

Mom said, "Now when you find her, apologize to her about the group." But I never did find Cynthia on the boat.

So then I woke up; it was 4:28 a.m. I called Jeannie, and I knew she would be getting ready for work. After I told her about the dream, I let her know that it was time for her to leave this job. The fear I felt was about her safety on the job. After I talked to Jeannie, she said, "Thanks, Red, for the call, and I have been thinking about retiring from this job. So this was a confirmation of what the Lord had shown me in the dream." She continued, "Okay, let me get ready for work."

I said, "Okay, be blessed today." Then I waited for a day to call Cynthia about the dream. I asked her to come to the hospital. I told her the details of the dream, then I apologized to her for any wrong that I'd done in overriding the vision that God had given her. "God placed help around you to be helpers to the vision but not to take over the vision. So for this reason, please forgive me. The Lord said, 'What I have placed in each of you when you come together, it will edify the people. No one is greater than the other. But we are to stay in our own lane and stand at our post to be able to do our part when it is the right time.' Cynthia, Mom told me she wants her girls to sing together. So let's do this for Mom."

After I was obedient to the spirit of God, I felt more sensation in my feet. I finally got it. When you work the word of God, then God's Word will work for you. Three weeks went by, and they were still doing tests on my legs to find out why I couldn't walk. I was still meeting people to encourage them that in this walk of life, our extremities are God's opportunity to show in our life and guide us out of our situation. I would let them know to have faith that God would see them through any obstacles.

The Lord gave me another dream. I went to church for a wedding. As I entered the corridors, there was a man, little in stature, but his voice was strong and loud. He was preaching, "The bridegroom is coming. But the people are not in position for the wedding."

As I entered the sanctuary, people were complaining, murmuring, and talking about the preacher. "Why is He out there preaching? This is supposed to be a wedding." Everywhere I walked, they were angry and complaining all over the church. As I walked around the church and ended back at the front door to escort the bride in, the people got louder and louder.

When I opened the door, instead of the bride coming in, the preacher came in, still preaching, "The bridegroom is coming." He grabbed my hand and pulled me behind Him as we walked around the church. He told the people, "You all are out of order and out of position. You are murmuring and complaining about Me preaching the Word instead of praising God for the Word. For it was the Word that redeemed us back to our creator." As the preacher and I walked around to the front of the church, He said, "My people, you are to line up with the Word of God. Usher in the Holy Spirit to lead and guide you." I looked up at the choir stand, and it was full of children. They were saying, "Holy, Holy, Holy, Greater Christians." The preacher held up His hand and beckoned for the children to come to Him. As they came before Him, He reached down and came up with a bottle of oil. He told the children, "Go and pour the oil in the church. For the church needs to be cleansed of all unrighteousness."

I said, "You want them to pour the oil in the church?"

And the preacher said, "Yes, pour it in the church. The church needs to be cleansed of all filthiness, and all blemishes, all murmurers, and all complainers. Pour the oil into the church, and let the church follow the preached Word of God. Not wavering to the left nor to the right. Just stand on the naked truth inspired by God. I, God, pour out to you. I walked on water. I opened blinded eyes. I gave wine for your parties. I've raised the dead. My people, believe these words. You will reap what you sow. My people, when are you going to live by the naked truth? Yes, pour the oil in the church. For My Word says, 'If my people which are called by my name would humble themselves and pray, and seek my face, and turn from their wicked ways, then will I hear from heaven, and I will forgive their sins, and I will heal their land' (2 Chronicles 7:14). You can't hold on to the old ways of man and expect to receive the blessings of God. We must renew our minds to think like Christ. Think and act as children of God. God said, 'My people, I set you on a hill to be light.' Remember this: you are in this world, but you are not of this world. You can't do as the world does. You shouldn't give that which is holy to the dogs. So if you are a child of Jesus Christ, then you must let the light of God shine in you wherever you may go. And whatever circumstances you come in contact with, acknowledge the Lord on how to conduct yourself so you can stay right with Him."

Now I understand that we should be obedient to God's Word and believe that there is nothing good our God will withhold from us. For He said in His Word that if you abide in Him and His Word abides in you, then you can ask what you will, and it will be done unto you (John 15:7). I believe it without seeing it, for God has chosen the foolish things of the world to confound the wise (1 Corinthians 1:27). So I know that the deeper I went inside myself searching for that much-needed love, the more hurt I was feeling, and I was wondering if the Lord heard my prayers. He let me know that some prayers are answered right away, like Peter sinking in the waters as he was walking to Jesus, but he lost his focus, and he said, "Save me, Lord." And immediately, he was saved from drowning (Matthew 14:22–31). Also, when Mary and Martha were praying for Jesus to come because their friend Lazarus, their brother, was sick, Jesus waited four days after Lazarus died because God's purpose was for the people to know that He is Jesus Christ, and beside Him, there is no other God. Their prayer was delayed but not denied. So I started believing God's Word. I believe there is nothing good that our God will withhold from us, for He said in His Word, "If you abide in me and my word abides in you, then you can ask what you will, and it shall be done unto you" (John 15:7).

Now if it sounds like I repeated myself, well, I did. One thing I have found out is that if God's Word is good enough to speak once, then it's good enough to repeat again and again. So now I know that for me, getting back on my feet will be delayed but not denied. So I decided to be obedient to God's Word and whatever He tells me to do. I learned that we can't let our dilemmas stop us from doing our Lord's work. We must realize that He is God, and if He brings us to the troubles and trials, He will show us a way out of the troubles and trials. We must do it in God's way. We have to choose ye this day whom you are going to serve. Then repent for our iniquities. As I made a complete change in my mind, body, and soul, the Lord moved on my behalf. He said, "I want you to do what you are called to do."

I said, "Lord, what if they don't accept me as a bold, preaching woman?"

He said, "Give My Word, for it will accomplish what I sent it out to do. My Word will not return unto me void. If they don't accept you, it's not you whom they don't accept. It's My Word that they don't accept, but it's up to me to chastise. You just love My people."

I said, "Yes, Lord."

So then the Spirit of God led me to talk to my cousin, Minister J. Wills, pastor of Mt. Hebron Baptist Church. He came to see me at the hospital. I was sitting up in bed when he came in.

He said, "Hi, Reggie. What happened?" wiping a tear from his eyes.

I told him, "Don't cry because it's not what it looks like." I continued, "God allowed this to happen to me to get my attention. But all is well because He's talking to me and He led me to talk to you." I asked him to help me understand. "Why doesn't the Minister's Alliance accept women ministers? If there's a soul to be saved, and you give God's word of salvation, and I give the same word of God, are you going to help me bring this soul to Christ, or are you going to fight me because I'm a woman?"

He said, "Reggie, I don't have an answer."

"Well, the Lord told me to tell you, 'And I entreat thee also, true yoke fellows, help those women that labor among you and that labored with me in the gospel, with Clement also, and with others, my fellow laborers whose names are found in the book of life.'" So I told my cousin, "Only what you do for Christ will last. Are you going to please your Ministers Alliance, or are you going to follow God's Word?" I continued, "Just do what God said to do, and God will take care of the rest when He comes back."

He said, "Okay, cousin Reggie, I accept this from you, and I want to see you up soon." I told him that when God said so, it would happen. But right now, God was doing work on me and through me in my mind, my body, and my spirit. I believe in God's Word, and He promised that I'll be back on my feet. He said, "Okay, Reggie, I love you," and he left.

The Lord kept talking to me, and He said, "Queen Re', don't let anything and no one separate you from my love. This love I placed deep inside of you is sacred and precious. And when I raise you up again, I want you to stand on the foundation of truth and be a bold soldier in the army of the Lord. Tell my people of this triumphant victory only because of being obedient to my word."

Now, I didn't walk out of the hospital, but after being in the hospital for about a month, I walked out. Only because I believed God's Word without looking at my circumstances. Now I feel a deeper love for everyone. If anyone doesn't love me or has a problem with me, guess what? It's their problem, not mine. I've got to be about my Father's business, so I don't have time to lose focus on God. I've learned that I have to be smarter than a serpent, to be wise, and to notice the enemy when he is present to trap me. I have been appointed to be anointed and empowered because the enemy is depending on my ignorance. The less I know, the more the enemy advances. But the more I know of the Word, the less the enemy advances. For we know that knowledge is power.

All of this was a personal experience for me to know God for myself and to accept Jesus as my Lord and Savior, also to let the Holy Spirit lead and guide me to the truth. I now hear God's voice. I feel His presence as I walk, and His Spirit walks in me.

Jesus told me, "As I sit at the right hand of my Father God, who is clothed with majesty, strength, and power, you, my daughter Queen Re', are clothed with wisdom. Not as the world gives, but as God the Father, God the Son, and God the Holy Spirit give unto thee. That you shall not be moved, for you are like the tree planted by the rivers of waters. You are rooted and grounded in the Word of God. And as you love Me, give this love to all and tell them to share this love all across the nation. My daughter, Queen Re', do you know who you are?"

I said, "Yes, Lord, I know, I know who I am now. I know to whom I belong. I know that I have a man that loves me. He will never leave nor forsake me. I know that He will love me like He loves the church. I know He will never hurt me. He lets me know in Him I live and move and have my being. And through Him, I can do all things through Christ who strengthens me. What a man! What a man! What a man!"

I tell everyone who has breath in their body, "You're only breathing because of the Lord God. Give yourself to the Lord and then repent of your sins, and He will forgive you. If you confess with your mouth that the Lord Jesus was born to a virgin, He lived and died, and believe in your heart that God raised Him from the dead, thou shalt be saved." My man Jesus has given me this deeper love, and this love I now live for. As I've learned during this one-on-one encounter with God, I've gotten closer to the Word. I also found out that the whole duty of my life is to fear God, which is to be respectful of His Word. "For thou shalt have no other God before Me." We are to keep His commandments:

1. To love the Lord thy God with all thy heart, and with all thy soul, and with all thy mind, and with all thy strength.
2. To love thy neighbor as thyself.

You keep these two commandments, and you would have kept all the laws. Now we're not under the law anymore, but we are under grace and truth. God said, "I change not. I am the same as yesterday and forever. My words don't change. I come to add to My Word, not to take away." So as His Word was from the beginning, it is still His Word today. In 2020, His Word still reads and means the same as the beginning.

So I (*we*) have to be obedient to His Word, to submit myself in the presence of God and in the presence of His people. It is okay to humble myself under the mighty hand of God that He may exalt me in due time. I must forgive myself for not loving myself. I now cast all my cares upon Him, for I know He cares for me. So I will stay dressed up in the whole armor of God because the adversary (devil) is still walking about seeking whom he may devour. I now know the grace of God has called me into His eternal glory by Christ Jesus. And after suffering for a little while, Christ has made me perfect, which means completely saying yes to God's ways. For His Word says, "Be ye therefore perfect, even as your father, which is in heaven, is perfect" (Matthew 5:48). What does it profit a man to gain the whole world and then lose his soul? People are choked with the cares, riches, and pleasures of this life and bring forth no fruits to perfection. They gain all that the world has to offer, yet they have not tended to the feeding of their souls for everlasting life. Believe this: we are not on earth to stay. We must prepare ourselves for the second coming of Christ Jesus and be ready to go back with Him when He returns. The choice is ours to make: to choose between serving God or Satan. Now is a good time to act. I've chosen Christ Jesus, and He has established, strengthened, and settled me. He has entrusted me with the task of letting His people know that the enemy is seeking whom he may devour. The devil comes with the same tools. Different looks but yielding the same destructive results. He comes to steal, kill, and destroy, and he will lead you further than you are willing to go with him. He will keep you bound, chained, and in despair all the way to the lake of fire. I tell you to seek Him while He may be found. Call upon Jesus while He is near. Let the wicked forsake their ways, and the unrighteous person their thoughts. Our ways are not like God's, and neither are our thoughts like His. But if you would submit your-selves unto Jesus and return unto the Lord, regardless of what you have done or said, return and repent, and the Lord God will have mercy upon you.

Despite what you have done in life or what you have said (as long as they do not include blasphemy against the Holy Spirit), return to Christ, repent for your sins, and Jesus will forgive you and have mercy upon you. Let us give thanks to our God, for He will abundantly pardon. The Lord said, "For as the heavens are higher than the earth so are my ways higher than your ways. And my thoughts are higher than your thoughts" (Isaiah 55:6–9).

So I advise whoever reads this book that it is not meant to tear you down but to build you up, helping you understand who you are and to whom you belong. You are all my brothers and sisters, and we all belong to Jesus Christ, who shed His blood, a price he paid for our redemption back to God. My brothers and sisters, there is no gender when it comes to the Lord. His Word is for all and to all. He gave His blood so that no one would perish, whether they have accepted Jesus as their Lord and Savior or not yet done so. Jesus said, "Let the wheat and the tares grow together, and I will do the separation when I come. I'm married to the backslider. Don't dwell on what you have done. Just come back to Me. As long as you have breath in your body, you still have a chance to accept Him as your Lord and Savior."

God made us in His image—the image of the Father, the image of the Son, and the image of the Holy Spirit. Three entities but one body. We are all different but still one body. Right where you are in your life, Christ will come to you. He'll come to your problem and solve it, for He is a problem solver. He'll come to your distress and provide comfort. He'll come to your pain and show you a way out. If you accept Jesus into your life and give your soul to Him, He will show up and lead you out of your misery. Don't exist in the form of hell, only to die and awaken in hell. Make a change right now by believing in your heart that God presented Himself in human form. He placed that seed in a virgin named Mary, and she called His name Jesus. He died, rose from the dead, and now lives, sitting at the right hand of His Father, God. We too can live again with our Father God if we would only repent of our sins. We can rise up, be saved, and live an eternal life with God forever. So I say again, choose today whom you will serve. Make your choice while you still have a choice; otherwise, if you wait too long, the choice will be made by God.

My brothers and sisters, it's time as never before to assume the right positions. Men, God is the head over you, and He made you the head over women. You are the head and not the tail. You are God's kings. Men, do not live beneath yourselves in this world but live as men of God. Do not allow the world to push you back into slavery. Our ancestors were told to pull their pants down so they wouldn't run from their masters. So I say to our kinsmen, if you are one of God's kinsmen, and you want to represent our King Jesus, I ask you to please pull your pants up and walk in the authority of our King. Men, as you run this race with God and stay in position with Him, He will direct you on how to move in this position. He will also show you how to love God's women as queens and prepare your children as heirs of this kingdom. He will guide you on how to live in the world but not be of the world.

Now to my sisters: women, let's get back into our positions and let the man take his rightful place. I know that before the ball stops bouncing in any situation, we will pick that ball up and keep it bouncing. We know we're not the head, but guess what, we're not the tail either. God said women are a helpmeet to our men. Let's help our kinsmen stay in position with God. Women, don't talk our kinsmen down or put them down. We must hold them up before the Lord to win the race that God has orchestrated.

My brothers and sisters, I write these things not to shame you but as God's beloved sons and daughters, He said,

> I warn you. For though ye have ten thousand
> instructors in Christ yet have ye not many fathers.
> For in Christ Jesus I have begotten you through
> the gospel. Wherefore I beseech you, be followers
> of me. (1 Corinthians 4:14–16)

Whenever you follow flesh that is not yours, it's a case of mistaken identity driven by emotions.

We should not allow the behaviors of this world to entangle our minds, spirits, and emotions, keeping us in the mess we're in and thinking we are truly living. We have to come away from living in the world. Drinking alcohol, smoking, fornication, idolatry, adultery, lying, murdering—these things must cease. Otherwise, we would be known as the walking dead. It's as if you know about Jesus but refuse to live by His Word.

> For the law in Christ Jesus hath made us free from the law of sin and death. And this is the Spirit of life. For what the law could not do in that it was weak through the flesh, then God sent his own son in the likeness of sinful flesh. And for sins condemned sin in the flesh that the righteousness of the law might be fulfilled in us. Who walk not after the flesh but after the spirit. (Romans 8:24)

So we must know that we are connected to God through the precious blood of Jesus. We are heirs and joint heirs with Jesus. You know how having a joint account at the bank requires both signatures? Well, Jesus has joined with you, and He signed this joint account in blood, His blood. It is signed, sealed, and delivered. No matter the impossible situation you find yourself in, His Word will not lie, and it will not return to Him void. His Word will accomplish what it is set out to do. You must know who you are and to whom you belong. Remember, you don't have to tolerate what the enemy puts before you. You're not the first to go through this, and you won't be the last, but you hold on to God's unchanging hand, or should I say, hold on to His unchanging Word, as He brings you up and out of the pits of mess. He said, "I'll never leave you nor forsake you." So if the Lord allowed you to be at this troubled bridge, then the Lord will give you victory over this troubled bridge. Just stay in God's will and be about His business.

All these words I'm giving you came to me first. So I had to apply them to my life so I could stop walking dead and begin to live in Christ to live again in heaven. But you don't have to wait to get to heaven to receive blessings. You can have blessings on earth as it is in heaven. I realized this wasn't about the me I see in the mirror every day but about the me, the image of God living inside of me. I had to make a change from the me in the mirror that danced the night away, prostituting through the church. I wasn't on the corner, but I was behind my own closed doors. But God told me, "You might seek and hide down here with every move, but I have an all-seeing eye that sees everything you do, the good and the bad." Now I'm not telling you this of myself so you can laugh and talk about me. I'm telling you this to shame the devil. The devil doesn't want me to share how Jesus has set me free from the bondage of fornication. Yes, I've been called names such as Holier-than-Thou, Self-righteous," or Ms. Nun. It used to hurt my feelings when they called me those names, but if that's what people saw, then to God be the glory. I know I live to please Christ, and He deserves all the glory and praise. We want people to see Christ in us, and that's what they see. So I don't get upset anymore about the name-calling. Now I believe my search for love is over. The search for love that I sought, God had already placed it inside of me. I just had to wake up that love by feeding that love and nourishing that love to live that love. Now I live to love, and I love to live as God's virtuous woman. I can't be bought for my price is far above rubies. So I say to God be the glory and dominion forever and ever. I completely say yes to God's will. And I completely say yes to God's' Word which is well pleasing in His sight. Now unto Him who is able to keep you from falling, to present you faultless before the presence of His glory with exceeding joy. To the only wise God our Savior, be glory and majesty, dominion and power both now and forever. Now I know without a doubt that *Jesus* is my love. Yes, *Jesus* is my deeper love.

Just Existing

I thought I finished writing and that my book was ready to be processed. But when my partner, Mrs. T. Toles gave me my book back, she stated that I wasn't finished. I knew exactly what she meant. I finished the book in December 2013, and I couldn't write anymore because it was so painful. I knew I had to write about the next years of my life, including my mom's life. What I felt inside was totally different from how I looked on the outside. I was in so much pain because my mom wasn't just my mom; she was my dearest friend, my confidant with whom I had the utmost respect. I stayed close to my mom to learn how to be a good mom myself. I was able to call my mother blessed because that's what I saw. My mom and I talked a lot, or rather, my mom talked, and I listened a lot throughout the years. I knew how to be a good daughter because my mom had taught me so well during her life. But since my mom went to be with Jesus, I've realized that I'm no longer just a daughter; now I'm a mom and a grandmother. I'm mad, hurt, and angry, and I feel so lost. I don't know myself anymore. What am I doing? I'm not a daughter anymore. Mom, talk to me. I don't know how to do this without your guidance. That's how you taught me to live because you have always been my mother.

I heard my mother tell me, "Live your life to please God. You won't and can't go wrong when you acknowledge Him in all your ways. He will direct your path. Don't stay upset and angry for too long because God wants to talk to you." This was my mom talking to me. Believe everything that He said. And believe I'm not far from you. As long as your heart beats, I'm just a heartbeat away. Tell the story as I gave it to you."

My mom was born on December 25, 1928, in Jackson, Mississippi, to Emerson and Elizabeth Cain. Emerson was the son of Sissy Griffin. Now Sissy had a twin sister named Missy Griffin, who was the grandmother of the Williams Brothers of Jackson, Mississippi. This made my mom, the Williams Brothers, and Huey Williams of the Jackson Southernaires second cousins. There were also Mr. Archie and Mr. Lawrence, but I forgot the other names she told me. They were known as the Mississippi Blind Boys. They would come to my mom's house to practice and sing. Even outside on the porch, they would start singing acapella, and my mom would blend right in with them. She was surrounded by all this beautiful singing in Mississippi. However, they had to leave Mississippi for the safety of my grandmother. Let me tell you this: My grandmother had only one dress that she wore to church every Sunday. Well, one day as my grandmother was crossing the street, a lady approached her and said, "Ma'am, you don't know me, but there is a woman who is trying to put a hex (witchcraft) on you to get your husband." She lifted the hem of her dress and showed her a piece of her dress had been cut out. She told my grandmother that, to break this curse, she must cross the waters.

She went home to explain why they must leave Mississippi. Mom really didn't want to leave. She was enjoying her life in Jackson, and now they had to move across the waters. And so they did. They crossed Mississippi waters into Ohio in the year 1945. Her new life in Ohio began. She met people, and some became her friends. She met Rosie Henderson, who got her to sing with the Starlights. She then met and married a man named Buster and divorced him as fast as she married him. Years later, she met and married Henry Frost, who changed her life tremendously by singing with his group, the Famous Jubilee's of Dayton, and having his children.

Later, her friend Rosie took her to meet with a group called the Morning Stars to audition. This group originated from Georgia and came to Dayton for a service. They then returned to Georgia to relocate the group to Dayton, Ohio. Mom then became their lead singer in 1948. As the years went on, Henry didn't like that Mom was singing on Sundays so much and not spending time with him.

So one Sunday, they had a heated argument about this. Mom finally gave in and didn't go to the program with the Stars. She ended up at a bar sitting with Henry. Later, Henry called Rosie and told her, "You all can have Baby" (that's what he called Mom). "She is so miserable sitting here with me." Mom left the bar and went where her group was singing. She also left Henry. She was tired of trying to please him, and she was not appreciated.

The Morning Stars traveled all across different states, singing and praising the Lord. Mom had nine children between the years 1951 and 1965, and she said she was tired of living like this. So in 1967, I remember hearing my mom praying and asking the Lord to forgive her for the way she was living. She said, "Lord, change my life so that I don't live to please man, but that I live to please You, Lord. Please, Lord, I don't want to do anything that will displease You and cause You to be separated from me. So please, Lord, help me to change." And I saw Mom change in a way that I was able to look upon her not just as my mother, but God allowed me to see my mom as a virtuous woman of God. I didn't know about a virtuous woman, but in 1967, God placed one before me for me to see and learn from her life. So she didn't just sing about Jesus but also studied Jesus with the Bible class of Salem Missionary Baptist Church, led by the late Pastor T. D. Moragne. She was also one of the musicians at the church. She lived a Jesus-centered life at home before her children.

As the years went by, there were some ups and downs. In 1966, Mom met Mr. Robert T. Lewis. I didn't like him at first because he wasn't my dad. He had a leather strap that he carried around with him, and if anybody sat in his chair, he would use it. But this chair was our chair before he met my mom, so I had a little resentment. However, as the years went by, and this man showed nothing but love and respect to my mom, I couldn't do anything but love him because my mom was happy. In 1972, he moved us into a new home and married my mom in the same year. Robert T. Lewis became my father. He was a good father all the way to the end when the Lord called him home in 2000. We love Mom, but we couldn't fill this void of her missing Daddy.

In 1982, Mom left the Morning Stars and started singing with her daughters in the Heaven's Unlimited, founded by my sister Cynthia Davis. We sang and went everywhere, releasing one album and two CDs. Now in 2008, Mom was sicker than usual. I called her doctor, Dr. Adegbile, to be seen, but he never answered. I finally got through to his office and found out that her doctor had abandoned her without a letter or a call. She had been with him for over fifty years, and this was how he treated her. I wanted to sue him, but Mom wouldn't let me.

Mom was getting worse, and while we were rehearsing one night, preparing for a service, Mom asked my baby sister, Cietha, to take her spot until she got back on her feet. As we were singing, Mom rose off the bed and said, "I think this is Mom's last year with you all."

We stopped singing and looked at her, and we said, "Ah, Mom, why would you say that?"

Mom said, "I just feel it."

I said, "Oh, Mom, we love you, but God has the last word, and I'm not ready to see you go."

So as we continued with the rehearsal, we were working on a new song, and Mom said, "That's not right."

We laughed and said, "Sick or not sick, Mom still knows when you're singing wrong or right."

I said, "Mom, from the way we sound, I think we need to cancel the service at Progressive Baptist Church." Mom said, "No, don't cancel anything. You all go and sing and give God the glory."

I looked at my sister, Cietha, and told her, "You can do this. Whenever you lead, just think of praise and worship, and you won't go wrong."

She said, "What if I sing off-key?" I said, "The anointing will put you back on key."

And as we practiced every week, Mom would let us know when we were singing right or even singing wrong. After one of the rehearsals, Mom stated she would like to hear the Canton Spirituals of Mississippi. This was one of Mom's favorite groups (her other favorite group is Mr. Spencer Taylor and the Highway Q.C.'s). I said, "Let me see if I can find a CD of them."

Mom said, "I mean, I want to see them live."

I said, "Oh."

The next day, I received a call from Jackson, Mississippi. It was Esther Wooten, the Canton Spirituals' booking manager. I didn't get a chance to call them, but God was orchestrating this situation. So I told Ms. Wooten about Mom's illness and that Mom wanted to see Harvey L. Watkins. Ms. Wooten said, "Harvey stated that one of you girls said you would bring him to Dayton." I told her that was me. And God made the way for us to bring one of Mom's last wishes.

When Mr. Harvey got to Dayton on June 19, 2008, Mom was so weak that she couldn't go to church. Mr. Harvey and the Canton Spirituals as a whole came to the house and gave Mom a private service before he came to church. My family couldn't thank God enough for making this wish come true for our mom. And we can't thank Mr. Harvey enough for the love that he had shown our mom. This wasn't the first time Mr. Harvey had shown us love. Ever since we started going to the Ecclesia Quartet Convention, founded by the late Roy Wooten and his wife, Esther Wooten, Mr. Harvey would always cook BBQ for us on the Saturday of the convention. Okay, he did it for the convention, but he still made you feel a personal love. And when he heard Mom sing, he told her, "I want to hear Heaven's Unlimited when they get more than ten minutes to sing. Now they are what you call professional. They do three songs within ten minutes."

Mom stated to us she wanted to go back to Jackson, Mississippi one more time. Mom was so happy when we went to the convention in March 2008. It was in Jackson, Mississippi. We saw a lot of our cousins. We even went to Brookhaven to see Mom's first cousin, Masaree. When we got back to the convention, they were calling our name as the second-place winners for 2008. Not knowing this was going to be the last time Mom got to go back home to Jackson, Mississippi.

So when Mr. Harvey came to Dayton, I didn't expect anything less than the love that he had always shown. So my family (Frost-Lewis-Green) wants to thank Mr. Harvey L. Watkins Jr. again for showing love to our Mom. We thank God we were able to fulfill this wish for our mom.

Thirteen days later, after the June service, Sis. D. White and Elder M. White came over to see Mom. She said, "Sister Reggie, the day my mom passed away, Mother Lewis came right over, so I have to be here." We did not know this was the day Mom was going to take her flight with God.

As we were talking, I began to look down on Mom. Her breathing was very shallow. Her breath lingered longer before she would take another breath. Her eyes were going back in her head, full of fluid. I raised her up and held her in my arms like she was a child. I saw my sister Toni do this a couple of nights before. So I said, "It worked then, it's got to work again." I said, "Mom, breathe, breathe, Mom, breathe, breathe. Please, Mom, breathe." And Mom took her last breath in my arms on July 2, 2008. It seemed like I lost it. I couldn't think.

My son, Antwann, called the paramedics. They said, "Lay her flat on the floor."

I said, "I'm not putting my mom on the floor."

Sister White said, "Sister Reggie, let your son lay your mom down."

As Mom lay on the floor, I began to do CPR, or what I thought was CPR.

Elder White said, "Sister Reggie, I don't think you're pressing on the heart."

I cried out to Elder White, "You do it. I can't take this," and I ran upstairs to the third floor. I was trying to find the papers that Mom signed because she didn't want to be revived by a machine.

She always told me, "When God is ready for her, He will come and get her, and she doesn't want to be held back."

I couldn't think; my mind was locked up. I didn't want to think anymore. It was like I didn't want to experience or accept what my mind had seen. I didn't want to live anymore. I was so hurt, mad, and miserable—all those feelings at the same time. I've never experienced this feeling before in my life. Losing a mother's love hurts all over your body.

As my sister, Cietha, came back home from work and the other sisters, Toni, Cynthia, and Angela, came in, and they began to clean Mom and prepare her body to be picked up. Oh, the love they showed during Mom's departure. I was no good at this moment; it felt like I was suffocating. I started taking extra breaths; I don't know why. Maybe I was trying to breathe for my mom. I was giving in to what I was feeling inside. I really didn't know how to feel. I just wanted the Lord to take me away.

I stayed on the third floor; I didn't eat anything up to the day of my mom's service on July 12, 2008, a day after my birthday. We sent Mom home in a Holy Ghost–filled celebration at the Potter's House Church. We thank our friend, Pastor M. McGuire, for the love you showed our family. I said to myself, "Mom, your life has touched many people because this church is filled to capacity." I remember you telling me that in our lifetime we're going to touch people's lives. It's going to be either positive or negative according to how you live your life. So I believe your life was a positive touch.

After this Holy Ghost service, we were getting ready for the cemetery, but a blind veil came over me as I entered the family car. I couldn't open my eyes to see. One of Mom's pins I wore fell off; someone picked it up and said, "I got it for you, Sister Reggie." My sister Toni took me out of the family car and got someone to take me home because I couldn't see. When I got home, someone helped me upstairs to the third floor, and that's where I stayed. I never received my mom's pin that I dropped at the service.

Since then, I have been hurt, angry, and even mad at God for taking my mom. I had always told the Lord if it was ever between me or my mom to go, please take me first because I don't think I could make it without my mom. But I guess God had another plan to show me.

As time went on, my seconds became my minutes, my minutes became my hours, my hours became my days, my days became my weeks, my weeks became my months, and my months became my years. I had stopped praying and reading the Word of God. I even stopped preaching.

The first year rolled around, the second year, the third year, and even the fourth year rolled around, and I was still full of anger. I would go to church every Sunday and put on a smile through my tears, give hugs through my hang-ups, and give kisses through my chaotic behavior. I was so disarrayed, and confused, and no one could get to my hurt to comfort me. And when I left church and went home, I would end up back in my bedroom asking God to take me. I was a mess, sitting there from sunup to sundown, day in and day out. I didn't want any communication with anyone. One day I heard the voice of the Lord, and He asked me, "What are you mad for? I told you I'm coming for My people Now are you ready?"

I said, "Yes, Lord."

He said, "Not with that attitude. Your mother was ready, now you get ready and stay dressed and ready so when I call your name, you can answer the call."

Something came over me, and I began to feel like the woman in the Bible who was in a bent position (Luke 13:11–17, a daughter of Abraham. She was special and precious in God's sight. God allowed her to be used, to be struck with a spirit of infirmity for eighteen long years. She couldn't straighten up. Some might have wondered what sin did she commit to receive the illness of this handicap. But I speak from experience in this position. God told me I was not present at the meeting when Satan asked to touch me. God allowed this to happen to me and told me that I have enough of His Word inside me to stand and not fall to the enemy. At the end of this example, it will prove the belief that God is the almighty, true, and living God, and there is no other God. Just as God healed this woman of eighteen years of suffering with this handicapped spirit on a Sabbath day, I also believe that my change is going to come.

God brought to my remembrance how I was physically bent over in the year 1976, but as God straightened my body up on the outside, my inside was still bent. But God was still working on me all the time. He was running me. For He knew of the seed that was planted in me. But along the way, I allowed a lot of interference to come in and stunt my growth. Even in the year 2014, I've let people and substances cloud my judgment of thinking to the point where

I wanted to leave this world. Yes, I thought about suicide. I couldn't deal with life and the complications of life. I was feeling sorry for myself because my mom and dad were gone. I felt doubled over with the cares of this world. I felt like I wanted the Lord to take me. I said, "Lord, I know you see me struggling. I know you see me swaying back and forth."

And God said to me, "I have planted a seed inside of you which is My Word. My Word is planted deep like a tree planted by the rivers of water, and you shall not be moved. You might be troubled on every side, yet you are not distressed. You might be perplexed but not in despair. You might be persecuted but not forsaken. You might be cast down, but you're not destroyed. All this is done for you to know that the life of Jesus might be made manifest in your body. They might call you weak, but God has made you strong. A strong tree is still standing. You might have lost some of your leaves on your tree. You might have lost some of your branches, but most of all, Jesus didn't let anyone tear you down. He knew what you could bear. Now if Jesus chose to use someone special like Abraham's daughter to prove a point to the people, then she was in the best of hands. The question is, wouldn't you want to be in those same hands?" My answer was yes. This God that changes not, I put my trust in Him, that He can keep me and sustain me. I'm not in good hands with Allstate, which is my insurance name, but I'm in good hands with Jesus, which is my assurance name. Yes, it was Jesus who had covered me through all my ups and downs, my ins and outs. It was Jesus who chose me. He trusted me to go through this task. God allowed this to happen to me so that He could get the glory. For as this is my will to do the will of God. And in doing His will, I will come out as pure gold. So now six years after my mom has passed, the Lord has let me know that I don't have to exist anymore, but I can live to live again.

As I'm writing these words, God is placing inside me a peace that surpasses all understanding. I can't explain the what, the where, the how, and the wishing; all I know is that I feel it deep inside, filling up the void I had. For the pain of remembrance that I hold inside of my mom. God said, "Remember the pain no more, but remember her laughter and her smile." The fear of forgetting I didn't want to let go because I didn't want to forget my mom. But God said, "Release and let her go. I don't give My people the spirit of fear. Forget not these things which are behind, but it will help you to press toward the mark of the future. Forget the pain and fear because the pain and fear are suffocating your faith. Just remember her songs that were songs from her heart. They will bring you laughter and a smile to last you a long while." I had so much work to do that I hadn't done because of this pain and fear. But now it was high time to get back to reading God's Word, praying again, preaching again, and teaching God's Word, standing in the faith and the anointing. And when I would be done, all to stand anyhow, I know that God would get the glory. No matter what the giant looks like, our God is greater. For greater is He that is in me than he that is in the world. So we stand in faith and with the anointing that destroys the yoke of the enemy.

So as a daddyless daughter, don't hate yourself or misuse yourself. Don't have so much anger that you spread the anger, hurt, and shame to your children, your friends, or your neighbors. You must get to the root of a problem so your problems won't keep stirring up in your life and taking over your life. I heard what mom had told me about my dad, but I just didn't think this hurt had affected my future. Mom always had told us if your dad ever needed you, then go and be a help. She would never talk my dad down to me. Although I was a daddyless daughter, Mom said, "Don't look to men to validate you as a woman. And don't let men misuse your body to validate yourself. Respect yourself, and others will respect you. Choose wisely who you spend time with. For you have no time to waste, and your time is too precious, just like you. You are worthy to be loved 365 days a year. But one day of existence is a long, long journey seeking love.

It's 2020; it had been twelve years since Mom passed on, and it still felt like the day I was holding Mom in my arms. I was still taking extra breaths as I thought of her. But God said, "I have her in my arms." So now I had comfort knowing Mom is in the arms of the Lord. That's my peace. If you have any loved ones that you think might be leaving Earth, make sure their soul is right with God before they leave this side of Earth. This is the most important part of life.

Despite what I see or feel, God promised to give me a peace that surpasses all understanding. So I have to hold on to His Words and believe it without seeing it. For I know God's word won't return to him void. Now no matter what, I know God's word will accomplish the very thing it is set out to do. So I will, and I must hold on to the hope with faith that God has eased the hurt and the pain and not to forget but to remember my mother's life. I now live and enjoy life without existing and feeling miserable inside. I have experienced God and accepted God yesterday. I have experienced God and love God today. And because I've accepted and loved God, then God will take care of my tomorrow. It's because of this experience I've died once, and I don't have to die again. Now I don't feel like I'm existing, but I do feel like I'm living to live again. Thank you, Mom, for teaching me to say, "Yes, Lord," and to accept the Lord in my life as my Lord and Savior. I'm now addicted to God's love. As you have given unto me, Mom, I now give unto my children and my children's children. That they will know and feel there is no other love deeper than the love of God. Mom, this love will bring us back together one more time for eternal life. So until then, this love is for you. I just want to thank God for coming where I was in my misery, in my hurt, in my shame, in my pain; I was just existing. But the Lord God reached way down and pulled me up. Then He placed my feet on a solid foundation. So now I don't have to be down or look down anymore. I know I can look up to the hills, which cometh all my help. For all true love comes from the Lord who made heaven and earth.

My question to you is this: Do you want to be covered by God's love? Then you must accept Jesus as your Lord and Savior. Repent from your sins; love God and everyone. Then and only then will your yesterday, today, and tomorrow all be covered forevermore. Then you will experience a deeper love. I pray this book of experiences will be an enlightenment to your life. That it will direct you, my brothers and sisters, to live unto God's Word as you experience a deeper love.

And now, my brothers and my sisters, I don't have to feel like committing suicide anymore. I don't have to exist anymore because God's Word told me to be strong in the Lord and in the power of his might. Now I can stand as I have on the whole armor of God to stand against the wiles of the devil. I'm able to withstand the evil days even in the year 2020. And when I've done all to stand, I would stand therefore in God's love, joy, peace, long-suffering, faith, gentleness, goodness, meekness, temperance, kindness, humbleness, so you won't be tricked by the enemy as I've gone through my tasks and trials of experiences.

My brothers and sisters, I pray that you be strong in the Lord and walk in the spirit and the characteristics of God. So that you shall not fulfill the lust of the flesh and of the world. But be ye followers of God as dear children. Let us walk in love as Christ also hath loved us. So when we all see God's face, He will say, "Well done, My good and faithful servant. Come on up, I'll make you rulers over many." So let us live in God and not exist in this world.

Your True Identity

Who are you? You must know who you are. Plus, you should know who you belong to. For we do not belong to ourselves. Our life was bought with a price, a price that we could not pay, so Jesus paid the price for us to redeem us back to our Father God. Our God made us as one but also made us differently. And until we all come together in God's love and compassion, just like the disciples in the upper room had to get on one accord to receive the Holy Spirit, we too have to get on one accord to receive the fullness of God that He has restored in us.

My brothers and my sisters, you've got to know who you are. Take an apple, for example. It's smooth on the outside, but inside, you might have some sour, some bitter, some sweet, and some rotten parts. But it's still what God made it to be—an apple. Now deep inside of the apple is the seed. The seed of the apple produces more of the product. Now look at yourself. God created man from the dust of the earth and breathed the breath of life into his nostrils, giving man life. The seed He placed inside of us is deep. So you have to go down inside of yourself. Go ahead. Look deep inside, past the hurt, the stumbling blocks, past the marrow and bones, past the pain and the anger, past the arteries and veins. Look deep, deep inside. You must get to the image. Do you see Him? Oh yes, that's the image that God placed inside you and inside of me. You must get to the image to wake Him up. Shake Him with the power of God that He placed in you from the beginning. You've got to get to the seed way out into the deep. You might have to fight to get to it but get there. You might have to cry along the way, but God said He'll bottle up your tears. Get to the seed and speak life unto yourself as you shake yourself.

And you tell yourself that you will live and not die because Jesus lived and died and rose again for you to live. Tell yourself, "Jesus lives for me, Jesus died for me, and Jesus rose for me so that I might have the right to the tree of life. Jesus did it for me." Why? Because our Father God loves us. Those who have accepted Jesus as their Lord and Savior and those who have not accepted Jesus yet. Jesus gave His life so that no man would perish. May the grace of God help you by empowering your mind to do the will of your Father God. Because when you line up with the will of God, you will do whatever is pleasing to God.

Before you act or do anything, you should acknowledge God's Word to direct you on how to move in any situation, for God's eyes are in every place, beholding the good and the bad. So He sees everything you do. Above all, we should want to please God, for He is the reason for our breathing. Let your mind be renewed in Christ Jesus so that your soul can reflect the Spirit of God's image as you love God's people. Knowing who you are, for everyone is unique, and know that no one can wear the shoes that Jesus made for you to wear. Everything and everyone has a purpose in life, so each of you should know your purpose to stay in position with Christ. Do whatever God has called you to do. And when it's time to live that eternal life in that new heaven, we will be at peace in that prepared place with our heavenly Father. That place that is prepared for God's prepared people. All God's people, know who you are by getting to know the image inside, for this is your true identity.

In Memory of My Fathers

Henry Neal Frost, April 29, 1920–February 1993
Robert Thomas Lewis, June 9, 1927–February 13, 2000

The love of his heart
I'm writing these words about Robert Lewis, my dad
He came into my life at the age of nine, he was a dad I didn't have
My mother loved her nine children, and of course, her singing and
    her love for him he caught
He decided to marry my mom despite what others thought
He worked third shift sunshine, rain, sleet, or snow
He went many times sick with no lunch but he knew he had to go
Sometimes he had to borrow money just for gas so he wouldn't miss
    work
Because he said, "If I miss one day, my family will definitely hurt"
Now when my mother's sister passed away, she had four children
People wanted to split them up but Dad said, "We'll take them all in
They've missed their mom, and all they have is each other
And if you split them up, they might lose contact with one another"
So we were fifteen in the house, Dad worked until he couldn't work
    any more
He would take light jobs to keep some funds coming in the door
It seemed like the more he worked, the less he got because of the bills
    he had to pay
But reading the Word of God every morning and seeing Sydney with
    the TV remote seemed to brighten Dad's day
As of this moment, February 13, I have to accept this day, he's home
    going with a smile

A smile of peace that will last a very long while
He passed on to his new home, there to share God's love and joy
God loved you most, Daddy, I'll miss you both, but I have to let you go
I'm Mr. Henry Frost's daughter from a physical spark
And I'm Mr. Robert Lewis's daughter from the love of his heart

Your daughter,
Regina/Queen Re'

In Memory of My Mother

Cloria Mae Lewis
December 25, 1928–July 2, 2008

I didn't dream of this story, but I wanted to write it down and tell of
    God's glory.
And to tell what my mom had imparted to me.
Such a virtuous woman, a godly woman indeed.
Mama was a fiery jewel in my eyes.
Her hand in mine her love from the heart I felt inside.
I stayed around my mom to be like my mom—loving, caring,
    thoughtful, and kind.
Mama always said, "It is easy to have lip service,
But be careful of things you say or do, and always keep Christ in your
    heart and on your mind."
Mama said, "What comes from the heart will reach a heart.
So think twice before you let it depart from your heart."
Well, not only did I listen and hear my mother's words,
But I watched her and became a doer of God's word just like her.
Mama lived to please God and lived to raise sixteen children.
Praying that what she taught will be pleasing to God and passed on
    to the other generations
One thing in serving God, Mama would never let anything get in the
    way not even the sickness
She'll say, "God is using me one more time, this day through this
    illness."
In going through, it was as if Mama conquered the hurt just to bless
    us one more time.

"I'm giving to each one of you according to the richness of mine."
Now these words came from my mom as she called me to her bedside.
"I want you to know I love you for you always taking Mama for a
    ride."
As she put her hand in mine and said, "I want you to be happy, so
    such as I have Reggie, I give unto thee."
I closed my hand as she moved her hand out of mine.
I said, "Thank you, Mama. I love you and God will show me what
    this means in his own time. You were a very good mom, you
    shared your love from your heart. Mama, we will take care of
    Gregory so you can answer God's call."
The Bible asks a question in Proverbs, chapter 31 and verse 10.
Who can find a virtuous woman? And my answer is my mom is one.
Her name is Cloria Mae Cain Frost Lewis down here on earth,
But being with God your name won't matter, brothers and sisters, we
    are and God is still first.
Now for peace's sake, this such you gave me, Mom will provide
    faithfully.
With love, joy, peace, kindness, goodness, gentleness, and God's
    mercy toward me.
We love you, Mom, and we'll miss you tremendously.
We can't hold you 'cause you're away so far.
But I will remember your words in song and deeds because it was the
    love from your heart.

Your daughter,
Regina/Queen Re'

To All My Siblings

Mom and Dad taught us to love and respect each other, no matter how different we all are; we are still one. As we unite with our different gifts together on one accord, God will open up the windows of heaven and pour out a great blessing that we do have not enough room to receive. We will not let Mom and Dad's teaching on the love of God be in vain. In this love, stay humble. With this love, stay dressed from head to toe in the armor of God. Let us all finish the race that is laid out for us. Let us do what God has called us to do to cross the finish line in peace with God. Let us stay *right* with God so we won't get *left* by God when He returns for His people. Let us change the things in our lives so we won't pay the price with our life. I love you all with a *deeper love.*

Your sister,
Regina/Queen Re'

The Image Inside

There was a boy who loved painting so much that his mom took him to the art museum to see the different paintings. As they were walking, the little boy wandered off by himself, and his mom didn't know where he had gone. The little boy came upon a man who was painting a picture, but as he got closer to the man, he saw that the man was blind. He was so fascinated by this blind man's painting that he sat down. Then he asked the man, "How are you painting if you're blind?"

The man said, "I have the image inside." The man continued, "Let me tell you a story. There was a man who lived, died, and was buried, but He rose again after three nights from a borrowed tomb. He got up with all powers in His hands. And because He lives, you can live if you accept Him as your Lord and Savior."

The little boy started laughing. The blind man asked him, "Why are you laughing?"

The little boy said, "Because your picture looks funny."

The blind man asked him, "What do you see?"

The little boy replied, "There are two men, and between the two men is a door. On one side, the man is standing at the door holding the doorknob, but on the other side of the door is a big red heart, and the man looks like he's knocking at the door, but you forgot to put a doorknob on that side of the door."

The blind man said, "No, I didn't forget the doorknob. I told you I have the image inside. As the man is knocking on the heart, He is waiting for you to turn the doorknob and open up to Him. Now I tell you that God is knocking at the door of your heart. Why don't you let Him in? Jesus said, 'I'm the door, and by Me, if any man enters, he shall be saved and shall go in and out and find pasture. If you are heavy-laden with the cares of this world, let God in, and He will give you the rest of what is needed for your life.'"

As the blind man designed the picture, God has designed our lives. We haven't really seen ourselves. But our Creator wants us to see ourselves through Him. This is the plan to have a relationship with Him, for it is He who gives us life and that more abundantly. So to you who are searching for a deeper love, I say to you, seek first the love of God and His righteousness, and all things will be added unto thee. For you can't find or get any deeper love than the love of God. Now is the time to answer the knock at the door of your heart.

I Choose a Deeper Love

I choose to forgive myself for not loving myself.
I choose to forgive myself for putting myself in harm's way for the
enemy to use.
I choose to love every one of God's people.
I choose to be obedient to God's Word.
I choose to value others as myself as they will see the light of God
in me.
I choose what I allow to come into my circle.
I choose not to be a fool who despises wisdom and instructions.
I choose to fear the Lord for this is the beginning of knowledge.
I choose to let nothing and no one interfere with God's product.
I choose to love instead of hate in this world.
I choose peace instead of war on earth.
I choose joy instead of sorrow in this world.
I choose Jesus instead of Satan.
I choose to live my life in the unmerited favor of God.
I choose to believe in the new covenant of grace, for with God, it's
already done.
I choose to receive what I believe in God's Word.
I choose to live in the manifestation of what I believe.
I choose Jesus, for He said in Joshua 24 in the fifteenth verse, "And
if it seems evil unto you to serve the Lord, Choose ye this day
whom ye will serve, whether the gods which your fathers served
that were on the other side of the flood or the gods of the
Amorites in whose land ye dwell. But as for me and my house,
I choose that we will serve the Lord."
I choose not to forsake the Lord my God to serve other gods.

I pray you to choose as I have chosen.
I pray you to choose *Jesus*
Jesus a *deeper love*

Sincerely,
Regina/Queen Re'

To All God's Children

Just because we fall doesn't mean that we are failures. We have to get back in our lane and finish the race God has set before us. We must endure until the end. The race is not given to the faster runner, nor is it given to the strongest person, but it's to all who endure to the end. Then and only then will you receive your reward. God has called you, and He has chosen you for a purpose. Remember we are overcomers of many things, but it takes God to deliver us from them all. For things such as a little headache or even as big troubled circumstances of the world, our God is bigger and greater. Our God will and can deliver us from them all. God wants His people to live free from bondage, so come away from the drugs, even abusing yourselves with prescription drugs as I did. The Lord said, "Come from the medicines because it's killing you." As the Lord told me, I now tell you. We might not have the planes or boats to bring the drugs in, but just because they put it in your backyard doesn't mean you have to use it or sell it to your brothers and sisters and kill them just for money. Also, come away from the guns. Why take someone's life when you can't give life back? God's word said, "Thou shalt not kill." What goes around will come back around. Be careful what you say or do because it will return to you like a boomerang.

My brothers and sisters, come away from alcohol. The enemy wants to keep our minds clogged and foggy so we can't think for ourselves. Let this mind be in you that is also in Christ Jesus. Only what you do for Christ will last. We will pay the price for the deeds that are done in our bodies. Whether sober or drunk, we will pay for our actions. So don't take anything that takes control of your mind or your body. My brothers and sisters, let's come away from smoking, even cigarettes, just because it's a ruination to your body. It's a slow killer, but it's still a killer. God wants us to come away from all things of this world that are killing us. For we are in this world but not of this world. God wants His people to think smart. Renew the mind to think like Christ. Make a change to come to Christ. Come just as you are, and God's Word will accept you and cleanse you and sanctify you to set you apart from living as the world and begin you to live like the Word. We must come away from our sinful ways of the world and the things we do for the almighty dollar. We must sustain ourselves unto the Almighty God who will supply all our needs according to His riches in glory. His riches never cease. But the riches of this world are not going to last much longer. My brothers and my sisters, if we want love in our lives, we must first put on love. To know love is to know and believe in God, for God is love. Then you must love yourself; otherwise, you can't love anyone else. As you accept the love of God, He'll help you with yourself, He'll help you to get in touch with yourself, He'll help you to know yourself, He'll help you love yourself, and He'll help you to befriend yourself, then you can be a help to others. If we want our crown to wear in heaven, then we must pick up our cross down here on earth and follow Christ. Sometimes the cross might feel mightily heavy. The load that I might have to carry is hurt, anger, hate, loneliness, lying, persecution, bitterness, fornication, adultery, killing, witchcraft, and much more. No matter what your cross is, God is asking us to pick up our cross and follow Him. Don't focus on the load because He said He won't put any more on us than we can bear. You don't have to bear this alone. You've carried all this down through the years; now I'm telling you to come to me, and I'll lighten up your load. And if there is something that you just can't bear, the Lord said, "Give it back to Me, and I'll bear it for you."

Jesus stumbled with His cross as He carried it, bearing our sins and our iniquities. And He is still calling out to His people, and He'll help you bear your cross. For He said, "You don't have to bear this cross alone." He has placed someone in your life to encourage you that you can make it. Yes, we might stumble, and we might fall, but Jesus is our advocate, and we don't have to stay down; we can get back up. You don't have to stay in sin because Jesus paid the price for all our sins and shame so that we don't have to sin anymore. We are free from the burdens of sin. No more guiltiness. Just as Jesus rose on the third day from a borrowed tomb, you too can rise from the mess that you're in. Get up and stay in the race until you reach the finishing line to see Jesus. Jesus said, "I will not forsake you, so you are not alone."

If we can see that it's about what we believe, not so much what we know in Christ, then we can finally see ourselves from God's point of view. Yes, Jesus, let me see my life from my perspective. I was going to church each Sunday, singing in the choirs, playing the piano, and I thought this was living. Now God has positioned me in another area. He allowed something to happen to get my attention. And I was able to see clearly from another angle of life. I saw my life from another perspective, and then I realized I had to change my way of living, for I was walking dead among the living. My mind had to be renewed and restored to stop being overtaken by the enemy's trap and to see where he was leading me—straight to the lake of fire.

My brothers and my sisters, look into your life and see another angle of life. As you start seeing with the eyes from the image inside of you, then you will see it as God sees it. As you begin to pull off the old way of life and the old things you used to do, and you decide to do what is right in God, but you still feel the heaviness of your cross, just remember the heaviness is what you've been carrying all this time. And you gotta know the God that is in you is greater than he that's in the world. So this cross of yours, you can bear it because you're not alone. Although you might feel alone, just believe without a doubt that Jesus is right there with you, helping you through all your circumstances. This trial and test are to be a testimony for someone else to know that God can and God will bring you up and bring you out of all your iniquities. As you follow God's ways, He will direct your path. Don't keep putting all your energy toward what's wrong with you. Instead, renew your mind and work on what is right in you. So that the right man in you can grow up and be able to rightly divide the truth of life.

My brothers and my sisters, all God's children, as long as you have breath in your body, you have a chance to change and make your life right with God. Let us live now to live again, an eternal life with Christ Jesus. Let's receive God's deeper love and live blessed.

My brothers and sisters, don't give up on God, for He's right there in the midst of your situation, whatever it may be. You see, in your down settings, your loneliness, or even in your weakness, this is when the enemy comes at you, hoping to steal or destroy you. But ultimately, he wants to kill you. Don't listen to the empty promises the enemy tells you. He has nothing good to offer. He is the author of everything that is the opposite of God. Because he is the father of lies. Don't let him deceive you into foolishness. Let us have the confidence in knowing the one and true living God who gave His Son to pay a price for us to be redeemed by his blood. Because of this purchase, we can live free in Christ Jesus. Know that all things work together for the good of those who love God and to those who are called according to his purpose (Romans 8:28).

My brothers and my sisters, I pray you do as I did let your worries go, and trust God completely. We have no need to fear anything because God is in control of everything. Just face everything and rise up and walk. So since we are the called children of God, let's live in this deeper love—the agape love of God.

My brothers and my sisters, I love you with this deeper love, and you can't do anything about it!

Sincerely,
Your sister in Christ, Regina/Queen Re'

From Image to Image

Let us make man in our own image. I was living my life like the Bible said, to stay right with God. But I did not have a relationship with Christ. I was living a Christian life but felt lost, not knowing which direction to take next. I saw myself running, but there was no clear direction for me to follow. Then God said, "Let Me talk to you. I want you to know that I do love you, and I know you love Me too. But you gotta stop and know that I am God. You may feel alone, but I did not leave you alone. I left you a Comforter to guide you. Stop trying to lead the Comforter when you don't know which way to go. I promise that the Holy Spirit, the Comforter, will lead you on the right path. The Holy Spirit will protect you from all hurt and harm. You might feel some percussion, but the Holy Spirit, the Comforter, will take on the greater part of the task. His hands will lead you into the backyard of grace and mercy. For those who have entered into His rest have also ceased from their own works, just as God rested within seven days. I want you to get back into my Word like never before. Get back to reading and preaching; that's what I have placed inside you. Don't worry about those who don't want to hear you; just do what you are called to do. The seed I planted in you will grow and sprout into a strong movement. You may sway back and forth, but you will stand as the image I have placed in you. You will stand no matter what comes at you. Don't get weary; just know that I've got you.

In July 2013, Heaven's Unlimited had to go to sing in Toledo, Ohio, for a pre-anniversary service. We were carrying three other groups with us: the Humble Sons, Doug Toles, and Witness for Christ, and Pastor Frye and his lovely wife, Venita, were also traveling with us. We were leaving directly after the morning service. I was sitting on the organ at Emmanuel Baptist Church West. While the guest preacher was speaking, a vision came to me. I saw myself riding in a white van, and suddenly, the van started flipping. I heard a voice say, "Don't go."

The preacher started hollering, "The Lord won't leave you, nor will He forsake you."

As I came back to myself, I said, "Wow, Lord, what did that vision mean?"

After the service, Pastor Frye said, "I can't leave yet until I get the guest minister settled, so just leave me the address, and we'll meet you in Toledo."

I said, "Okay." I left and went to pick up the group and all of them who were riding in the van. Yes, it was a white van, but I hadn't thought about the vision I had while sitting on the organ. As we all gathered, we prayed and started out. We were on our way to have a blessed time in Toledo, Ohio. My brother Rev. Henry Frost and his family group from Ypsilanti, Michigan, were also meeting us there.

When we were about ten miles from Lima, Ohio, there was a construction area, and we had to slow down from 70 mph to 50 mph. Just as we passed through the construction area and I pulled over to the right lane, the Humble Sons passed us and four other cars went by. I still hadn't reached the 70-mph speed. The next thing I heard was a pop, and the van started going in every direction. I held on to the steering wheel so tightly. The van was going left and right, then backward and forward. Then it was headed for a ravine, and all I could see was clouds. My sister Toni hollered, "No, Lord, not like this," and the van turned and went sideways down the highway.

I was yelling, "Lord, You've got this? You said You've got this, Lord. I can't do this."

He said, "Hold on. I've got this." The Lord and I were having this conversation while all this was going on. I just let go and let God have His way. My hands were still on the wheel, but I didn't have control at all.

Toni shouted out, "Okay, Lord," and the van turned and started going backward into a shallow ravine and hit the side of a mountain.

There were eleven people in a fifteen-passenger van, and everything from the front went to the back. Throughout this ordeal, my ninety-six-year-old cousin, Rosa Lee Henderson Foster, was in the front passenger seat, but she slept through the whole thing until we hit the mountain. When we hit the mountain, my cousin woke up, and her wig landed in the front window. She said, "What was that?" I believe if the Lord hadn't let her sleep, she probably would have had a heart attack due to the accident. One thing I noticed was that God didn't allow any other automobiles to be in the area as we went through this ordeal. After we hit the mountain, two people drove up. The man was an off-duty fireman, and the woman was a nurse. They worked quickly to get everyone to safety.

The Humble Sons must have seen us in their rearview mirror because they were running back down the highway. Justin, Jacob, De'Andra, Ronald (Meme), and Leroy. They looked like a football team. They came and helped us get out of this smoking van. I'll never forget the love they showed Heaven's Unlimited. Nine of us had to go to the hospital. Thank God we only had bumps and bruises, and nothing major. We can't thank God enough for sending our friends Doug Toles and Witness for Christ, and Pastor Reginald Frye and his wife Venita. They showed their gratitude and love by helping. When we arrived at the hospital, I was telling some of them about the vision and how a voice had said, "Don't go."

A couple of them said, "You should have done what the voice had said."

But I told them that the voice didn't sound like God's. God's Word says, "My people know my voice."

But I listened to the voice that said, "I've got you. I will never leave you, nor will I forsake you." I believe that the voice I listened to was telling me, "Whatever you have to go through, just believe in Me."

> For my thoughts are not like your thoughts neither are my ways like your ways. I need you to just believe. Believe that if I bought you to the troubled bridge that I God Almighty will take you over the troubled bridge.

So I think the voice that was telling me to stay home was not God's. I think the enemy didn't want me to go so God wouldn't get the glory from my obedience. But I think God was preparing me to trust Him, to truly believe in Him, and to have faith in His word, from one image to another image.

As Jesus was faced with the cup of our iniquities, the crown of thorns upon His head, and the piercing in His side, He was whopped all night long, humiliated through the city carrying the cross. Stumbling and falling while carrying our sins, nails in His hands and nails in His feet. He was lied about. Jesus was faced with all this in the cup. The cup that God told His Son He must drink from, this bitter cup. Jesus prayed to His Father, "Father, I see all that is in the cup. Can You please take this cup from Me?" But this was part of redeeming God's people back to Him. Jesus then said, "Oh My Father, if this cup may not pass away from Me except I drink it, then Father, let Your will be done." Jesus was saying, "I'm doing the work of My Father, God. For I must do what I am called to do. My Father's Word is with Me, and He'll never leave Me, so I must do My Father's will no matter what I'm about to face." Likewise, we too, who are Children of God, must be about our Father's business and not our own business. Jesus said, "The things you hear of Me, do, then you do the same." Everything is not going to be a bed of roses. You might get lied to and talked about all through the city. You might feel like you're carrying a heavy load that's hard to bear. You may feel like your cup is overflowing with the cares of this world, but we must be about our Father God's business.

This Christian life is not like the hokeypokey. You put your right foot in, you take your right foot out, you put your right foot in, and you shake it all about, you do the hokeypokey, and you turn your life around—that's what it's all about. You're either in, or you're out. You're either hot or cold, but if you're lukewarm, God said, "I'll spit you out of My mouth." You have to choose whom you're going to serve, whether God or the devil. You can't be with God on Sunday, and then live as the world on Monday through Saturday. That's the hokeypokey life. We must do what we are called to do. As one image left, the other image is to house the Comforter.

When we were released from the hospital in Lima, Ohio, my brother Ronald, his wife Tammy, my son Antwann, and my daughter Zy'Atrice came to pick us all up and bring us home. Toni, Osby, Sheila, Peanut, cousin Rosie, Angie, Mariyah, Xyon, Judea, and Suwannya—there were eleven people. We thank our Lord and Savior for life, health, and strength.

Now as we were made in the image of God the Father, God the Son, God the Holy Spirit, our image was connected together.

> From image to image, abide in me as my word
> abides in you, then you can ask what you will,
> and it shall be done unto you. (John 15:7)

You asked a question: Do you have a good religion? Some might say, "Certainly, Lord." But I say, it's not a religion that is needed. The question should be: Do you have a good relationship? Stay in a relationship with Me while you're in this borrowed land. This land is not your home, just like Jesus borrowed a tomb from Joseph because he wasn't going to stay long. In just three days, He arose and went to His Father God, for His work was finished. So now we also must work until the Lord God calls us home. God gave us power so that we don't have to be slaves to sin ever again.

Let us stay connected to God through Jesus to live together in eternal life, from image to image. As Jesus, who knew no sin, took on our sins, Jesus, who is rich in everything, became poor for my sake. He changed places with me and placed me in prosperity instead of poverty. So as Jesus rose with all power, I can proclaim the power that was given me to speak life unto myself. For I'm the head and not the tail. I'm an overcomer. So I'm telling you to stay in a relationship with Jesus so that when you see Jesus, He will say, "Well done, My good and faithful servant. You've been faithful over a few things. Come on up. I'll make you ruler over many." From image to image. Now I must be about my Father's business, for His image has awakened me. His image is teaching me to talk to the image in you. From image to image, let us come from being conformed to this world. Come from being conformed to the devil's ways. But let us be transformed by the renewing of our minds. How? I'm glad you asked. By reading the Word of God, studying the Word of God, and eating the Word of God so that we become the light of God, we can be a help to others. So others can see their way out of their wilderness, out of their tests and trials, even their tribulations. As they see the image of God in you, it will give them hope to come from the ways of the world to see the image inside themselves. For the image inside of us tells us, "Thy will, O Lord, will be done on earth as it is in heaven." To be in the will of God is to be prosperous, to be strong, and to be healthy with joy. Bringing heaven on earth in a visible sense—oh, what a feeling. From image to image, I want to be healed, so I speak healing to myself.

Father God, I forgive myself for letting the enemy take control of me. Right now, the Holy Spirit has full control of this image. I forgive all who have done me wrong, for they know not what they do. And Father, I forgive all who came against me to stop my purpose. Father God, I thank You, for I now abide in You, and Your Word abides in me, and You said I can ask what I will, and it shall be done. Now as God the Father, God the Son, and God the Holy Spirit are one, then so are we one image to image.

Know this without a doubt that we are the children of God, made in His image to possess all the goodness our God has for us. Image to image, if you give, it shall be given unto you, good measure, pressed down, shaken together, and running over. Shall men give unto your bosom? For with the same measure you meet with all, it shall be measured unto you again (Luke 6:38). Image to image, what God has given us, we must also give to others to be a blessing. For hoarding the blessings of God is a human move, but giving as the image of God giveth, that's divine. For it is more blessed to give than to receive (Acts 20:35). Image to image, we've got to wake up. Yes, wake up ye dead bones, and know who you are. We have been praying and teaching our children, "If I die before I wake, I pray to the Lord, my soul He takes." This is not talking about a flesh sleep where you sleep so hard and miss out on what God has for you in this life to live in the next life. But this prayer is talking about a spiritual awakening to God's Word so your soul can live an eternal life with

God. Image to image, wake up. Being a victorious Christian is a full-time job. Don't be slothful in maintaining what you have gained of the word of God so you won't go back to being slaves of the enemy.

The fifth chapter of Galatians says,

> Stand fast therefore in liberty wherewith Christ has made us free and be not entangled again with the yoke of bondage.

Image to image, wake up. It's not time to think for yourself or sit back, kick your heels up, and look at television. It's time to get busy with our Father God's business. It's time to be witnesses to our brothers and sisters about the real godfather of the soul. The world said James Brown was the godfather of soul. But I disagree with this statement. The only thing James Brown could tell you was, "This is a man's world," or "Papa's got a brand-new bag," or "He's got soul, and he's super bad." But I'm here to tell you, if he didn't give his soul back to Jesus while he was still on Earth, then that is what you call super bad. You see, God breathed in our body, and we became a living soul. God gave us life, so that makes Him our Godfather of soul. God is the lover of my soul. He is the redeemer of my soul. For I believe without seeing. I believe I'm healthy. I believe I'm wealthy. I believe I'm prosperous. I can speak it and believe that it will come to pass, all because I'm the Image of God.

God's word says in 1 Thessalonians 5:4–10,

> But ye, brethren, are not in darkness, that that day should overtake you as a thief. Ye are all the children of light, and the children of the day. We are not of the night, nor of darkness. Therefore let us not sleep, as do others. But let us watch and be sober. For they that sleep, sleep in the night. And they that are drunk, are drunk in the night. But let us, who are of the day, be sober, putting on the breastplate of faith and love. And for a helmet, the hope of salvation. For God hath not

appointed us to wrath, but to obtain salvation
by our Lord Jesus Christ, Who died for us, that
whether we wake or sleep, we all will see him.

But we all will not live an eternal life with Christ unless we believe and confess that He is the Lord of our souls. Otherwise, you will spend eternity in the lake of fire. And don't let Him catch you being a liar, for a liar will not tarry in His sight. So image to image, let's wake up! From image to image.

Whose Job Is It

(Author Unknown)

This is a story about four people I read about. Their names are Everybody, Somebody, Anybody, and Nobody. There was an important job to be done, and Everybody was asked to do it. Everybody was sure that Somebody would do it. Anybody could have done it, but Nobody did it. Somebody got angry about that because it was Everybody's job. Everybody thought Anybody could do it, but Nobody realized that Everybody wouldn't do it. It ended up that Everybody blamed Somebody when Nobody did what Anybody could have done.

But now I say, don't let God call for you, and your work is undone. Do what you are called to do. Let us be about our Father's business. Let's get the job done. Be a witness for Christ.

Your Truth Is on Trial

In my college days, I was glad to be away from home. I felt free to go where I wanted to go and do what I wanted to do. I didn't have to ask for permission. I could make my own decisions about where, when, what, and how to live my life and ask why later. Much of what we think is the truth about ourselves is not always really the truth. My truth was to satisfy the desires of my flesh. But the real truth says it's not about a feeling; it's about having faith in knowing the true and living God, for His truth is marching on. Some of us wouldn't even recognize the truth if we heard the truth about ourselves. Jesus told Peter in Matthew 26:34 the truth about how he was going to deny Him three times before the rooster crowed. Peter said, "I'll never deny You. I'll die with You, Lord." But it happened just as Jesus said. Peter and the eleven disciples walked with Jesus (the Truth) but still didn't fully understand the truth. Many of us today have heard the Word, which is the truth and still have not fully accepted the Word as the truth. Jesus's truth was on trial as He stood in front of the governor, Pontius Pilate. Jesus could have prayed for His Father to send His angels, but He didn't. Why? Well, all this had to be done so that the scriptures of the prophets might be fulfilled. God's Word had to come to completion, for His Word will not return to Him void. His Word will go out and do what He was sent out to do. Pilate heard the truth as the truth stood before Him, but He still didn't know the truth. Even Pilate's wife told him that he couldn't find any fault in this just man. Pilate merely washed his hands and let the people decide what to do with the truth. Guess what? You're going to answer for yourself. You won't be able to pass it off to someone else to handle. You will have to answer for yourself because your truth is on trial. Our truth might tell us it's okay for women to be with another woman's husband. But Jesus's truth says,

> Likewise, ye wives, be in subjection to your own husband. (1 Peter 3:7)

Our truth might tell you it's okay to take a drink of wine. But Jesus's truth says,

> This cause was the gospel preached also to them that are dead that they might be judged accordingly to men in the flesh, but live according to God in the spirit cause the end of all things is at hand, so be ye sober and watch unto prayer.

Our truth might say, "Let's drink, party, and be merry." But Jesus's truth says, "Be not drunk with wine but be filled with the spirit of God" (Ephesians 5:18).

Our truth might say, "Love those who love you." But Jesus's truth says,

> Thou shalt love the Lord thy God with all my heart and with all my soul and with all my strength and love neighbor as thyself. For it is written on these two commandments hang all the laws. (Mark 12:30–31)

His commandments are not subjections but his commandments are for us to obey His word.

Whose report are you going to believe? Now is the high time to choose whom you are going to serve. Will you choose our truth to please the flesh, which will die soon, or Jesus's truth, which is marching on and will never die? Just as Jesus's truth was on trial, our truth is also on trial. For as much as Christ has suffered for us in the flesh, so we are to arm ourselves with the same mind. For He that hath suffered in the flesh have ceased from sin. We should no longer live the rest of our time in the flesh to the lusts of men but to the will of God.

Jesus's truth is marching on, and our truth is rising again. There is nothing hidden that will not be revealed. Let's do the will of our Father and let our truth march on. There will be many falling by the wayside. But the choice is yours to get up and return to your first love if you want to live and not die. Jesus's truth is marching on, and it won't stop for anyone. His Words and truth remain unchanged. For, he said,

> Blessed is he that readeth and they that hear the words of his prophecy. Blessed is he who keeps those things of his word and his truth.

As John wrote to the seven churches in Revelation signified His Word by His angel.

> Grace be unto you and peace from him which is, which was and which is to come. From Jesus Christ who is the faithful witness, the only begotten son of God, the Prince of peace, He's the king of kings. Unto him that loves us and washed us from our sins in his own blood. He hath made us kings and priests unto God and his Father. To him be glory and dominion forever and ever.

Jesus said, "Behold, I will come back on a cloud." And I know that every eye shall see Him. Every knee shall bow down before Him, and all kindreds of the earth shall wail because of Him. The corona came, and all the earth was suffering with death all over the world. We're trying to cover up with masks. We're staying at home not to be affected by the plague, but when God calls your name, you can't hide in the house; you have to answer the call. Other plagues are coming, and the only safest place is in the will of God. So repent, and come back to your first love, for His Truth is marching on. Let God cover you with His blood. And when the death angel comes, it will pass you by. Don't live as the world, for the world's truth says it's okay to marry the same sex, but God's truth destroyed the city of Sodom and Gomorrah because of the same truth. He's the God that changes not. If marrying the same sex was a sin, then it still is a sin now. God loves everybody, but He hates the sin we do. Since I have accepted Jesus completely, I've stopped sinning. Every time sin came my way, and it felt like I was getting close to fulfilling that sin, I would feel something in my mind that triggered down into my legs. It made me think about when I was paralyzed from the waist down, and I would stop because I didn't want to end up back in that situation of not walking. I don't indulge in sin. Listen, God's people, the enemy, the devil, is out seeking whom he may devour. The enemy knows our weakness, and that's what he puts before us. But God has given us the power to stand against the wiles of the devil. Listen, God's people, if you sin on earth, it equals death in eternal life. Don't think it strange that things are happening as they are. God had already told us what life was going to be like when He comes. It would be like in the days of Noah. People will be partying, marrying, and having babies. Men will also be establishing their own righteousness to live and please themselves, thinking they're doing the will of God.

So the Bible is fulfilling itself. Now are you going to fulfill the truth as a witness of God? Are you going to stand against the rulers of darkness of this world? Are you going to stand against the spiritual wickedness in high places? God's people, we are to stand with the truth in our mouths, speaking boldly as we humble ourselves unto God. Pray and seek God's face. Then turn from our wicked, sinful ways. For the truth you live is coming up again in judgment. And your truth will determine whether you live an eternal life in a new heaven or eternal life in a lake of fire. Your truth is marching on to where? That's the question! Change the things in your life so you won't pay the price with your life. Your truth will tell your story.

So You Thought I Was Through

My Legacy

No, I left a legacy to carry on.
Son, Antwann H. D. Frost
Vintage Frost Productions
Wife, Monica Frost
Monica's Designs
Daughter, Zy'Atrice S. E. Frost
YG Young Grandma Children
Ei'Zayah Haratio Frost
Xyon Jazzmyn Maree' Frost
Mariyah Zy'Ann Evans
Lyric Serenity Guy
Mykiece Richardson
Myiel Frost
Messiah Frost

I taught my legacy to be brave in this dangerous life and not to be scared or to fear those who kill the body but are not able to kill the soul. Instead, we are to fear God, who is able to destroy both body and soul. So my legacy stands with the courage of the anointing of Christ to do what you are called to do by the higher power. That is to love and live in Christ Jesus, to live again with Christ Jesus. Let's live this deeper love in Jesus and use the power that God has given us to trample over the enemy. Use the words of God, not the words of this world. The enemy will tremble at the name of Jesus. You don't have to accept what the enemy brings your way. Speak God's Words and live in this deeper love of God. For you are an heir and a joint heir with Christ Jesus. As God spoke it, and it was done, so shall we speak it and it shall be done. God has given us power and authority over Satan. So don't be discouraged and fearful of what the enemy is doing or has done. Stand firm on the Word of God. Speak the Word of God and command the enemy to flee. Let not your heart be troubled by what the enemy does. Jesus said, "As you believe in God, believe also in Him, Jesus." Be about God's business, which is to be a witness to others that God is real, and that He sent His Son Jesus, who lived, died, and rose again. Now He sits at the right hand of His Father, and one day we will be with Him, for He has prepared a place for His prepared people. So to my legacy, don't live to please people but live to be prepared for God, the Higher Power. Let's stay right with God so we won't be left by God.

Ei'Zayah Frost, reach for your destiny in God. You are more than what you were given. But what you have in your hand is enough for you to make it through life in Christ. Stay right with Christ and keep Him first in everything you do. Acknowledge Him in all your ways. As YG always prayed with you daily, this is what sustains you on earth. Having a relationship with Jesus so you can go back with Christ when He returns. What you lose on earth shall be loosed in heaven. So lose the goodness of Jesus, then you shall receive the goodness in that new heaven as well on earth. You already see some of the goodness. You received the MVP for the 2018 All-American Football in Alabama, and there's more to come. Don't stop. Don't give up if it gets too hard. Just keep pushing forward. Don't let your tragedies of life determine your future. Keep your eyes on the prize, which is in Christ Jesus, and you shall receive a just reward. Keep reaching for your destiny in music with your cousin Peanut. Through Christ, He'll be able to take you to the next level. I love you, and remember, change the things in your life so you won't pay the price with your life. Stay right with God so you won't get left by God.

Xyon Frost, you are my pretty brown number 3. You are smart, witty, a gourmet cook, a hairstylist, a dancer, a singer, and a drummer. You have a diversity of directions you can go into. I prayed with you daily to have a relationship with Christ as you choose your direction. I can't live my life through you, but I can give you the such that I have that was given from your great-grandmother (Cloria Lewis). The Holy Spirit that is within you will direct you if you let Him lead you. You've chosen Jesus as your Lord and Savior; now let Him lead you to your path of life. Love to live and live to love. Remember to stay right with God so you won't get left by God.

Mariyah Evans, you are my pretty brown number 4. You are smart, lovable, sporty, and unique in style; a dancer, singer, and drummer. Some may call you Erykah Badu, but I say be yourself whom God created for you to be, a child of God. All the gifts God gave you, don't misuse them, and give them to the dogs. Don't live in this world, although you are in this world. You are the gift as you give yourself to Christ, and God blesses you, then you should bless others and share your gift as God orchestrates you. Remember to stay right with God so you won't get left by God.

Mykiece Richardson, you might be little in stature, but the God in you stands so tall that your footsteps are destined for greatness. So much energy, loving, and sporty, and a professor in any direction that God leads you. You are a dancer, and you are unique in dressing. You're going to reach countless people in your life, so keep letting your light shine on your hill, so someone, anyone, everyone can see Christ in you and see their way out of their darkness. I love you, and remember to stay right with God so you won't get left by God when He comes again.

Lyric Guy, my darling princess. You are my model—unique, sophisticated, lovable, humble, smart, and respectful of self and others. The things I see in you—common sense, patience, love, and manners—show your character that money can't buy. Don't let anyone buy you to disrespect your character because you were bought a long time ago. You are a precious jewel and you belong to God. We look alike in spirit by the blood of Jesus, but you look better than me in the flesh. I love you, and stay pretty inside and outside. Remember this: stay right with God so you won't get left by God.

Myiel Frost, my brown sugar—a singer, a dancer, a comedian, and the *great finder*. When I think of you, I think of integrity, trust, class, manners, and much love. But even in all these beautiful things, they don't define you. For being blessed and being in your presence, your blessings spread out to all that are in your company. You are a very truthful person, which is very rare. The day we couldn't find the Uno cards, you told the truth and said you hid them because you kept losing in the game. You told me, "YG, you know I'm the great finder, just ask me, and I'll tell you where they're at." One day the great finder didn't feel well, she had a headache, so I prayed for her. Later, I came to her to see if she was feeling better. She told me, "YG, I don't think your prayer worked because you didn't pray with power."

I said, "From now on, I'll make sure that I pray with power." Out of the mouth of babes. So I took heed of her words to me: "Little prayer, little power; no prayer, no power." My brown sugar, remember this. I love you and keep praying. Remember to stay right with God so you won't get left by God.

Messiah Frost, I know you're new on the scene, but you have a job to do. As your father and mother teach you of the higher power in Christ Jesus, let the Holy Spirit lead you into your destiny. I believe you're going to touch a lot of people with the love, joy, and peace that the Higher power places in you. Always remember these words: stay right with God so you won't get left by God. I love you.

My Legacy

Look to Jesus, for He is the answer to everything. The answer was here before the problem ever arrived. The world is running out of answers to the equations of this world. But as we take up our cross and follow Christ Jesus, He will deliver us to that new heaven. My legacy, keep fighting the fight of faith that you've already won. Change the way of thinking like the world, for we're in this world but not of this world. My legacy, as you seek God first in every area of life and have a relationship with Jesus Christ, He will supply all your needs according to His richness in glory. I pray my life speaks for me and to you, that as I move upward, my legacy and my shadow are also being blessed as they move forward into their destiny. My legacy, live in this deeper love of Jesus Christ, our Lord. For we are fearfully and wonderfully made, and marvelous are His works that our souls know right well (Psalm 139:14).

My legacy, you have been set apart from the world and chosen to do the will of God. My legacy, embrace this deeper love, for only what you do for Christ will last. Let God's love reign inside of you, for it was Jesus's blood that redeemed us back to God. There will not be a session for the Whites, or a session for the African Americans, and the Mexicans, not a session for the Baptists, Catholics, or the Church of God in Christ. There will be no segregation. Everyone will be there together because of the blood of Jesus, as one. So, my legacy, do it God's way. We must live life in God's way. Love God with all your heart, with all your mind, with all your soul, and with all your strength, and love your neighbor as yourself. My legacy, love like God said love, and He'll take care of the rest. Anyone who has a problem with my legacy, it's your problem and not mine. My legacy,

God has begun a new work in you, and you will perform it until the day of Jesus Christ. I pray that your love may abound more and more in knowledge and in all judgment, that you may approve things that are excellent, being filled with the fruits of righteousness which are by Jesus Christ, unto the glory and praise of God (Philippians 1).

My legacy, as I lived to please Jesus in front of you, my princes and princesses, then you also live to please Jesus to be His kings and queens. This is my legacy; watch them grow. As I say to my legacy, I say to all let's stay right with God so we won't get left by God when He returns for His prepared peoples. Change the things in our life so we won't pay the price with our life.

The Lord changed my name to Queen Re'—a narrow beam of light, a gleam or slight manifestation: God hasn't shown me everything, but He has given me enough light to shine in my life, for my life to be fulfilled, for I completely belong to God—mind, body, and soul. I abide in God, and His Word abides in me; He promised I can ask what I will, and it shall be done. I didn't ask for a husband, but God thought it was time for me not to be alone. God sent me one of His kings, Mr. Jimmie L. M. Martin.

I told God in 2001 when it's time for this virtuous woman to receive one of His kings, let him tell me he's a good man. That way, I know that he was sent by you. And he did tell me on July 28, 2019; he asked for my number. I thought he was asking for my group to sing, but then he turned and said, "By the way, I'm a good man." I wasn't looking for a man; I was seeking Christ. At that moment, God released a love as never before within me. We married on July 18, 2020. We're in love with God and in love with each other. This love is deeper than no man can put asunder. We're looking forward now to what God has in store for us. It's not what man thinks about us that matters, but it's what God thinks about us; that's all that matters. However God chooses to use us for His glory, then we say yes and amen. He promised He'll never leave us nor forsake us, so no matter what the situation looks like, God is with us to take us to the other side.

This is to my brother Eddie Williams. I asked Cynthia to read to you the Ninety-First Division of Psalms. God has covered you as you walk through this valley of the shadow of death. You should fear no evil, for God is there with you. God will show us the way through our darkness because we can't see our way through darkness. We stumble and even fall, but hold to God's Word; it will see you through. Even in the light, we might have some dark moments, but don't give up or give in. God is still God, and His Word never returns to Him void. He's God in the good times, and He's God in the bad times. He promised He won't put more on you than what you can bear. Second Corinthians 12:9 says,

> My grace is sufficient for thee; For my strength is made perfect in weakness. Most gladly therefore will I rather glory in my infirmities, that the power of Christ may rest upon me.

Psalm 121:1 says,

> I will lift my eyes unto the hills which cometh all of my help.

John 14:3 says,

> And if I go and prepare a place for you, I will come again, and receive you unto myself; that where I am, there ye may be also.

So whatever you're faced with, Eddie, God has strengthened you to go through. So if He needs to use you this moment one more time, I hear you saying, "Here I am, Lord. I'm ready to be used by You." You are a soldier in the army of the Lord, and you are needed at the front line. You are armored from head to toe for this job that He picked you to do. You are ready, and you are not alone. As God was with Moses, David, Paul, and Silas, the Lord God is with you.

Hold your head up, soldier, so you will hear those famous words, "Well done, My good and faithful servant." Be obedient to the will of God, that He will get all the glory. The choice is God's, and whatever He chooses, He has strengthened His children to accept. Jimmie and I love you, Eddie Williams, and God's got you covered in every area of your life. For we are more than conquerors through Him that loved us.

This is to all who read this book: You will find no deeper love than the love of God. How deep is your love? If you don't have the love of God, then you need to search for a deeper love. Now this love of God is signed and sealed by God, and the search for this deeper love is now delivered.